THE GOLDEN YEARS

text: David Sandison, Michael Heatley, Lorna Milne, Ian Welch

design: Paul Kurzeja

Welcome to *The Golden Years* and your chance to look back at the comings, goings, to-ings and fro-ings which made 1967 such a fascinating year. While the year will forever be remembered by many as the one which gave us The Summer of Love, flower power, peace, love (man!) and a belief that the youth revolution really was about to change the world for the better, the truth was that the older generation was still busy finding new ways of messing it all up.

The Vietnam War dragged on, pulling more and more young Americans into its deadly embrace. Arabs and Israelis finally exchanged more than insults in a deadly six-day battle which saw Israel score a remarkable victory, though not peace. Military rebels in the Nigerian province of Biafra began a war for independence which they would ultimately lose. Australia lost a Prime Minister, Harold Holt, in a tragic accident, and the film world lost the larger-than-life figure of Jayne Mansfield and the supreme craftsmanship of Spencer Tracy. Konrad Adenauer, the man who'd steered West Germany back into a state of international respectability after the horrors of Nazism, also said his last farewell, leaving the world

stage emptier for his absence.

In Bolivia, the life of Ernesto 'Che' Guevara came to a violent end, only to start a cult movement which would long outlive the communist cause he espoused.

But there were triumphs too. Francis Chichester proved that eligibility for an old age pension was no bar to courage and skill when he steered his yacht around the world single-handed. Christiaan Barnard offered hope to future generations when he completed the world's first successful heart transplant.

Maybe it was the Summer of Love, after all......

JAN

JANUARY 4

Donald Campbell Dies In Bluebird Crash

THE PEACE OF THE Lake District's Coniston Water was shattered today when an attempt by British speed king Donald Campbell to break his own world water speed record went disastrously wrong. His turbo-jet hydroplane *Bluebird* was travelling at over 300 mph (485 kph) when the front end lifted, sending the craft somersaulting backwards into the lake.

Although Campbell's oxygen mask, helmet, shoes and mascot teddy bear were found at the scene of the accident, there was no sign of Campbell himself.

His previous water speed record - set on Lake Dumbleyung in Australia two years earlier - was 276.33 mph (440 kph), while the same year had seen him set a new land speed record of 403.1 mph (648 kph) on the Lake Eyrie salt flats in Nevada.

Born in 1921, Donald had followed in the wake of his father, Sir Malcolm Campbell, who was also the fastest man on land and water in his time. The engine used in the World War II *Spitfires* was developed directly from that which Malcolm Campbell used in his record-breaking drive at Bonneville Flats in Utah in 1935.

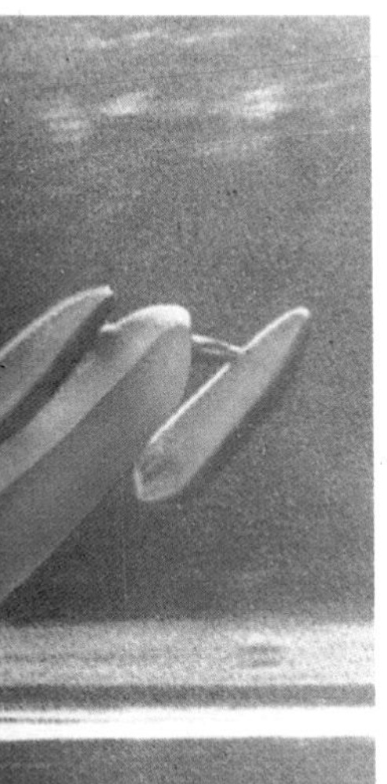

JANUARY 12

Clay Fails To Dodge Draft

Cynics could be forgiven for being just a little suspicious of boxer Cassius Clay's conversion to Islam. The heavyweight champion, who'd announced he wanted to be known from now on as Muhammad Ali and claimed to have 'no quarrel with them Vietcongs', recently asked the Louisville, Kentucky, draft board to exempt him from military service because he was now a Black Muslim minister. Unfortunately, the board today decided against reclassifying him.

Ironically, the boxer had originally been declared unfit for military service, having failed the US Army's aptitude test. But test standards were lowered as US involvement in Vietnam put more pressure on the armed services, so Ali was now eligible.

On April 30, he would be stripped of his world title for refusing to do military service, and would spend the next three years fighting an eventually-successful legal battle to clear his name and win the right to box again.

UK TOP 10 SINGLES

1: Green Green Grass Of Home
- Tom Jones

2: Morningtown Ride
- The Seekers

3: Happy Jack
- The Who

4: Sunshine Superman
- Donovan

5: I'm A Believer
- The Monkees

6: In The Country
- Cliff Richard

7: Save Me
- Dave Dee, Dozy, Beaky, Mick & Tich

8: Matthew And Son
- Cat Stevens

9: Any Way That You Want Me
- The Troggs

10: Night Of Fear
- The Move

JANUARY 15

Let's (Not) Spend The Night Together

The Rolling Stones' controversial new song *Let's Spend The Night Together* was aired for the first time tonight on US television's prime-time *Ed Sullivan Show,* but lead singer Mick Jagger appeared to slur the lyrics to avoid being taken off air.

The show's notoriously conservative host - who'd once insisted that a young Elvis Presley be shown only from the waist up to avoid inflaming American teenagers - had asked that the song's key lyric be changed. When challenged that he'd effectively sung 'Let's spend some time together', Jagger claimed he'd 'just sung mumble'.

Later in the year, on the same show, The Doors' lead singer Jim Morrison was asked to change or omit the line 'Girl, we couldn't get much higher' from their *Light My Fire* single, but ignored the request.

ARRIVALS

Born this month

12: Mark Moore, UK pop star (S'Express)

DEPARTURES

Died this month:

1: Moon Mullican, US 'King of Hillbilly Piano' (*Jole Blon, I'll Sail My Ship Alone*, etc), aged 57

18: Evelyn Nesbit, US stage and film actress, aged 81

21: Ann Sheridan (Clara Lou Sheridan), US film actress (*Angels With Dirty Faces, They Drive By Night, King's Row, Come Next Spring*, etc), aged 52

JANUARY 17

Grimond's Dream Is Over

Claiming that he was now too deaf to lead it efficiently, Jo Grimond resigned as leader of Britain's Liberal Party today, a position he had held for the past 11 years. Grimond entered the Commons in 1950 as MP for Orkney and Shetland and became leader in 1956, his priority being to transform the Liberal Party into the primary party of opposition, replacing Labour.

Although the period of his leadership saw a doubling of the number of Liberal MPs elected to Parliament, he handed over to the new leader, Jeremy Thorpe, with his dream still unrealized.

JANUARY 7

Classic Costume Saga Kicks Off

BRITISH TELEVISION viewers had a new, unmissable drama series to block-enter in their diaries today when the first episode of *The Forsyte Saga* was broadcast by the BBC.

The 26-part dramatization of John Galsworthy's epic novels was produced by Donald Wilson and screened in black and white. Initially broadcast on the so-called 'minority' BBC2 channel, its overwhelming success led to the series being repeated on the main network channel, BBC1, from September 1968.

Principal characters in what the British Film Institute called '21 hours of fine drama' included Soames Forsyte (Eric Porter), his first wife Irene (Nyree Dawn Porter), his daughter by second marriage Fleur (Susan Hampshire) and Young Jolyon (Kenneth More). Each of the 50-minute programmes was presented as a separate act, standing dramatically by itself, but building on the established plot. As this included the machinations of a prosperous Victorian family and touched on such controversial subjects as marital rape and the early fight for women's rights, *The Forsyte Saga* was bound to be a winner.

JANUARY 12

New Town For Britain

Plans were announced in London today for what would eventually be Britain's biggest new town ever, spreading over 22,000 acres of Buckinghamshire countryside some 50 miles north-west of the capital.

Milton Keynes, with main streets built on a US-style grid system, would incorporate several existing villages, together with Bletchley Park, where boffins cracked the Enigma Code during World War II. A network of cycle-ways would keep cyclists and motorized road traffic apart. But not everything in Milton Keynes was designed to be ultra-modern: in an echo of Stonehenge on Salisbury Plain, Midsummer Boulevard in the centre of town would align exactly with the rising sun at the summer solstice!

JAN

JANUARY 27

Inferno On Apollo Launchpad

The United States' *Apollo* moon project was set back almost before it had begun today when three astronauts - (pictured left to right) Virgil Grissom, Edward White and Roger Chaffee - were killed in a launchpad fire at Cape Kennedy. The three, who were undergoing a simulated launch for the first *Apollo* mission scheduled for next month, hadn't even left the ground when an electrical spark ignited the oxygen inside the cabin and a gantry outside the spacecraft prevented their escape from the burning capsule.

February's scheduled flight, in which the three astronauts were to have spent two weeks orbiting the earth, was to be the first manned mission of the *Apollo* project, NASA's entry into the so-called 'space race' with the Soviet Union to put a man on the moon by the end of the decade.

Just four days later, in Texas, astronauts William Bartley and Richard Harmon were killed when fire swept through a spacecraft simulator.

FEBRUARY 10

Insurance Con-Man Savundra Arrested

DR EMIL SAVUNDRA - (pictured) the fraudster *par excellence* who believed he was a cut above the rest - was arrested in London today, only five days after he'd returned from Switzerland to protest his innocence in a live TV interview with David Frost. He was charged with a number of offences connected with the collapse last year of his Fire, Auto and Marine Insurance (FAMI) company.

Around 600,000 British motorists (later described by an unconcerned Savundra as 'peasants') were left uninsured when the company collapsed with losses of over £1.5 million ($4 million). The swindler, who throughout his long career had suffered several 'convenient' heart attacks when facing yet another fraud charge, had already engineered elaborate frauds in Ghana, Costa Rica and Goa before ever setting foot in Britain, where he was first arrested for forgery in 1954.

Despite this track record, Savundra - who was born in Sri Lanka - had been able to set up FAMI simply by proving he had assets of £50,000. Offering comprehensive motor vehicle and health insurance for a fraction of the premiums charged by major companies, he'd paid himself more than £300,000 in the two years FAMI existed.

Tried and sentenced to eight years in prison, Savundra would die in 1976, from a last genuine heart-attack.

FEBRUARY 18

Farewell To 'Father of The Bomb'

Robert Oppenheimer, leader of the team responsible for building the US atomic weapons which helped bring World War II to its cataclysmic end at Hiroshima and Nagasaki, died today at the age of 62.

In 1942, Oppenheimer had been appointed director of the top-secret Manhattan Project which, at Los Alamos, New Mexico, developed the first atomic bomb. He did not, however, advocate its use against Japan, and had been one of a number of scientists who had advised against its deployment.

Oppenheimer subsequently became an outspoken supporter of joint international control of nuclear energy, an opinion which finally caused him to fall foul of the US Senate witch-hunt of Senator Joe McCarthy, and he lost his security clearance for sensitive research. However, his censure by the right-wing was not enough to destroy his considerable reputation as a gifted scientist and teacher, and in 1963 he received the Enrico Fermi Award.

FEBRUARY 3

Hit-Maker Joe Meek Shoots Himself

The introverted but often inspired British record producer, Joe Meek - the brains behind The Tornados' chart-topping *Telstar* and John Leyton's *Johnny Remember Me* - shot and killed himself today in his London studio.

One of the few independents in an era when producers tended to be tied to major record companies, Meek's innovative techniques made him the nearest Britain would get to America's Phil Spector. But, like his counterpart, he found that a lot of business complications went on behind the music. Meek, too, had suffered at the hands of an industry with which he refused to play ball, and had suffered the failure of his own label, Triumph Records.

A devoted fan of US rock star Buddy Holly, Meek shot himself on the eighth anniversary of his idol's death.

UK TOP 10 SINGLES

1: I'm A Believer
- The Monkees

2: Let's Spend The Night Together/Ruby Tuesday
- The Rolling Stones

3: I've Been A Bad, Bad Boy
- Paul Jones

4: This Is My Song
- Petula Clark

5: Matthew And Son
- Cat Stevens

6: Night Of Fear
- The Move

7: Release Me
- Engelbert Humperdinck

8: Green Green Grass Of Home
- Tom Jones

9: Sugar Town
- Nancy Sinatra

10: Hey Joe
- The Jimi Hendrix Experience

ARRIVALS

Born this month:

1: Mike Milligan, Republic of Ireland international football player

3: Tim Flowers, England international football player;
Mixu Paatelainen, Finnish international football player

17: Gary Fleming, Northern Ireland international football player

28: Colin Cooper, English football player

DEPARTURES

Died this month:

3: Joe Meek, UK record producer *(see main story)*

6: Martine Carol (Maryse Mourer), French film actress (*Caroline Chérie, Lucretia Borgia, Nana, Lola Montes,* etc), aged 45

8: Sir Victor Gollancz, UK book publisher, aged 73

15: William Bullitt, US politician

18: Julius Robert Oppenheimer, US nuclear scientist *(see main story)*

FEBRUARY 25

Boston Strangler Capture - Again!

Albert DeSalvo (pictured), the man known to millions as the Boston Strangler, was recaptured in a low-key arrest in a clothes shop in Massachusetts today, only a day after he'd escaped from a prison mental ward.

He entered the shop wearing a badly-fitting naval uniform and asked to use the telephone. After a while a shop worker asked him, 'Are you DeSalvo?' When he assented, the police were called.

Although DeSalvo was infamous for the assault and murder of 13 women in Boston between 1962 and 1964 he was said to have admitted, legal fine-print meant that he could not be tried for those offences. Instead, he received life imprisonment for other crimes he had committed. He was to die six years later in prison, when warders found him stabbed to death in his cell.

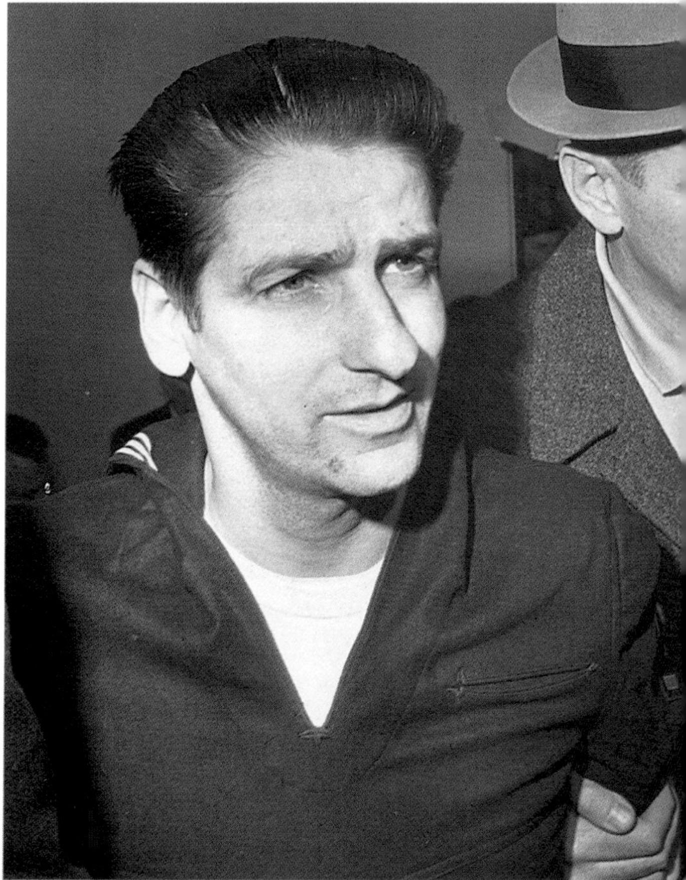

FEBRUARY 26

Vietcong Flee As US Launch 'Junction City'

MORE THAN 25,000 US troops launched the United States' biggest offensive of the Vietnam War today in an effort to find and destroy the headquarters of Nguyen Huu Tho, political leader of the Vietcong. Code-named 'Operation Junction City', the assault was made on the area known as War Zone C, and took the fighting very close to the Cambodian border.

Apart from its political importance, War Zone C was also believed to be the terminus for the Ho Chi Minh supply route from North Vietnam, and so was a strategic military target for the US paratroopers who - for the first time in Vietnam - were dropped into the action.

Reporters on the scene described skies filled with criss-crossing aircraft, thousands of parachutes dropping into the jungle, and a mass retreat by Vietcong forces taken by surprise and completely overwhelmed by superior manpower and resources.

FEBRUARY 13

Monkeemania Hits Britain

US pop group The Monkees, the first act to be manufactured for TV, were greeted by thousands of screaming teenagers when they arrived at London's Heathrow Airport today. The four-man group – Davy Jones, Mike Nesmith, Micky Dolenz and Peter Tork – had been created by pop mogul Don Kirshner to play in a TV series about their strictly scripted exploits.

Truth soon became stranger than fiction. Their first single, *Last Train To Clarksville,* had peaked at No 1 in the US last November, while they would eventually tour (on one occasion with Jimi Hendrix, unbelievably, as support) and write their own songs and play their own instruments before finally disbanding.

In the week ending February 4, The Monkees had completely monopolized the top spots in the US and UK album charts - *I'm A Believer* was a No 1 single in both countries, while their eponymous first album topped both LP listings. In the following week, they surrendered their US album chart dominance to...*More Of The Monkees!*

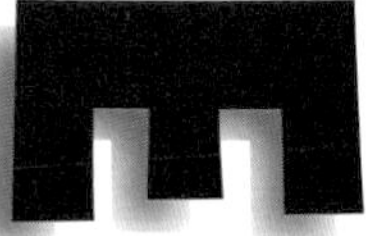

FEBRUARY 16

British Films Sweep The Globes

Two films which, for many, captured the essence of the Swinging Sixties – *Georgy Girl* and *Alfie* – today won Golden Globes in the prestigious Hollywood critics awards ceremony.

Although millions of ordinary girls could identify with Lynn Redgrave's Georgy, who found herself cast adrift in fast-moving 1960s London, it was Tom Springfield and Jim Dale's title song, performed by The Seekers, which gained the film instant recognition.

For 33-year-old Londoner Michael Caine (real name Maurice Micklewhite), his performance as Alfie, which also received five Academy Award nominations, was an impressive follow-up to his debut in *Zulu* two years earlier.

MARCH 9

Stalin's Daughter Defects To West

IN A GREAT PROPAGANDA coup for the West, Svetlana Alliluyeva, the daughter of Russian dictator Josef Stalin, asked for asylum in the United States today.

Officials at the US Embassy in New Delhi, India, were amazed when Svetlana – who had been secretly allowed out of the Soviet Union to return the ashes of her dead husband to his native India – simply walked into their building and announced her wish 'to seek self-expression' in the West.

Svetlana, who was 41, would be flown to the United States to begin a new life. While her father, who ran the Soviet Union with unmatched brutality from 1924 until his death in 1953, had been largely discredited by subsequent regimes, her defection was a blow to Soviet pride which the West would use to make great propaganda mileage.

MARCH 4

Winwood Gets Caught Up In Traffic

Stevie Winwood, one of Britain's most successful rock singers at the advanced age of 18, shocked the music world today when he confirmed that he had left the Spencer Davis Group (pictured), with which he'd sung since the age of 14. His elder brother Mervyn, better known as 'Muff', was also departing to become a talent scout and record producer. With Stevie doubling on keyboards and lead guitar, the two appeared on such international hits as *Keep On Running, I'm A Man* and *Gimme Some Loving.*

Two weeks later, British pop paper *New Musical Express* would report that the younger Winwood, now calling himself Steve, had already formed a new group with drummer Jim Capaldi, guitarist Dave Mason and sax-player Chris Wood.

The resulting outfit, known as Traffic, would become one of the most influential British bands of the psychedelic era, cutting hits like *Hole In My Shoe* and *Paper Sun* as well as a string of top-selling albums.

MARCH 1

British Troops Fire As Aden Riots

As fights between opposing political factions escalated into full-scale riots and a British woman died in a bomb attack on an official government dinner, British troops in Aden opened fire on rioters tonight.

The unrest followed the funeral of a local government minister who'd been assassinated. A crowd of 15,000 mourners turned on two Arabs who shot at the procession, chasing them on to the roof of a mosque and hurling them to their deaths.

As news spread, so did the number of running street fights between rival groups. Confronted with a mob who'd ignored repeated calls to disperse, the British soldiers opened fire.

MARCH 13

LSE Students Go On Hunger Strike

The appointment of Walter Adams, the former head of University College, Rhodesia, as the new director of London's prestigious London School of Economics was the cause of a protest by students who staged an all-night sit-in in support of two fellow students who'd been suspended for holding a banned meeting denouncing his appointment in January.

The protests escalated during the week that followed, with 13 students going on a hunger strike for five days during a mass occupation of the school's buildings by more than 1,000 protesters. The college authorities finally relented and the suspension order on Marshall Bloom and David Adelstein - the original 'martyrs' - was lifted.

UK TOP 10 SINGLES

1: Release Me
- Engelbert Humperdinck

2: Penny Lane /Strawberry Fields Forever
- The Beatles

3: This Is My Song
- Petula Clark

4: Edelweiss
- Vince Hill

5: Here Comes My Baby
- The Tremeloes

6: On A Carousel
- The Hollies

7: There's A Kind Of Hush
- Herman's Hermits

8: Georgy Girl
- The Seekers

9: Detroit City
- Tom Jones

10: Snoopy Vs The Red Baron
- The Royal Guardsmen

ARRIVALS

Born this month:

8: John Harkes, US international football player

15: Ian Ferguson, Scottish international football player

16: Terry Phelan, Republic of Ireland international football player

DEPARTURES

Died this month:

5: Dr Mohammed Mossadegh, Iranian politician, Prime Minister 1951-53, aged 86

6: Zoltan Kodály, Hungarian composer, teacher, aged 84 *(see main story)*

11: Geraldine Farrar, US classical soprano, aged 85

30: Jean Toomer, US writer, aged 72

MARCH 4

Underdogs Win Cup Final

Once dubbed 'Hardaker's Folly' after the English Football League secretary whose brainchild it was, the League Cup this year emerged as a major event thanks to its switch to a single Wembley final (from the previous two-leg affair) and the prize of a place in Europe for the winner.

Queens Park Rangers' stirring 3-2 victory over West Bromwich Albion today upset the form-book, as the Third Division side were two divisions lower than the team they beat. Rangers overturned a 2-0 half-time deficit to take the trophy, a victory masterminded by future England player Rodney Marsh. And although they were denied a European place due to their lowly League status, they consoled themselves by winning their division by a 12-point margin.

MARCH 26

New York Hosts 'Be-In'

Not to be outdone by the 'Be-In' hosted by San Francisco last year when thousands of prototype hippies filled the city's Golden Gate Park to tune in and drop out to music and poetry, like-minded souls on the US's East Coast mounted a similar event today in New York's Central Park. While ordinary citizens attended the city's famous Easter Day Parade, more than 10,000 young people bedecked with daisies and badges attended an alternative rally organized by a group of hip New Yorkers.

MARCH 6

Founder Of 'Kodály Method' Dies

Zoltan Kodály (pictured) Hungary's most famous composer after Béla Bartók, died today at the age of 84.

The son of a State railway worker, Kodály was – like Bartók – a champion of Hungarian folk music, incorporating its melodies, sounds and themes into his compositions, the most famous of which, his *Háry János* opera and orchestral suite were published in 1926 and 1927.

Although he continued to compose throughout his life, Kodály made an equal impact on the teaching of music, developing an innovative system, the Kodály Method, which is now in constant use throughout the world.

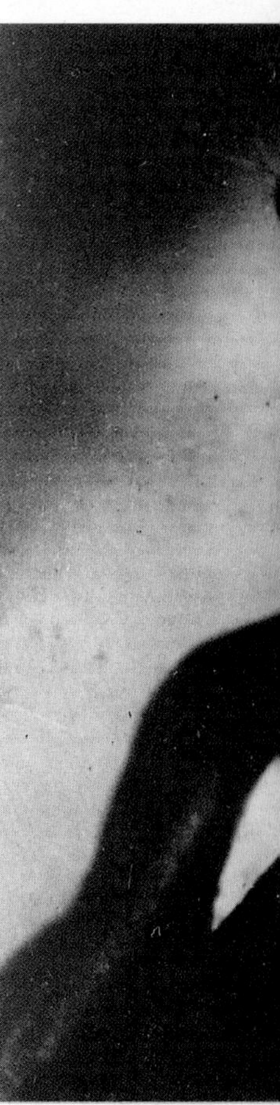

MARCH 19

RAF Jets Bomb Stranded Torrey Canyon

THE GREATEST ECOLOGICAL disaster Britain had ever seen began to unfold today in Cornwall when the 61,000 ton oil tanker *Torrey Canyon* ran aground on the Seven Stones Reef between Lands End and the Scilly Isles, spilling her cargo into the sea.

The accident, which broke the back of the supertanker to release 100,000 tons of crude oil, was blamed on a combination of mechanical failures and bad weather. It cost the lives of thousands of seabirds and would cover 100 miles of beaches with a thick black sludge within days.

A vast clean-up operation was launched amid fears that the slick would devastate the year's tourist trade. Initial attempts to prevent further spillage proved inadequate. An emergency cabinet was called by Prime Minister Harold Wilson, who had a holiday home on the Scilly Isles, where the decision was taken to set the vast oil slick alight.

On March 30, Royal Air *Force Hunters*, *Sea Vixens* and *Buccaneer* roared down on the stricken tanker, blasting her with 1,200 gallons of napalm and almost 50 incendiary bombs. While senior RAF officers were confident they'd eliminated the source of the vast slick, oil was reported to have spread across the Channel to French beaches.

GREAT FILMS MAKE OSCARS A TOUGH CALL FOR THE ACADEMY

A great year for movies, which meant a tougher than usual task for voting members of the Academy of Motion Pictures Arts and Sciences freed from the usual diversion of big budget stiffs lobbied into nomination by frantic major studios.

Only one of the five short-listed for the Best Picture Oscar fell into that category - the tedious *Doctor Dolittle* - which, in common with previous expensive flops powered into nomination in the vain hope that the publicity attached to an Academy Award would revive its fortunes, had no back-up nominations for its director or actors to justify inclusion in the Best Picture running.

That was not true of the real contenders, of course, and the Academy finally had the unenviable job of separating *Bonnie and Clyde* from *The Graduate, Guess Who's Coming To Dinner?* and *In The Heat of the Night.* Also up for consideration were the various actors and technical participants in 1967 films like *Cool Hand Luke, Camelot, The Dirty Dozen, Thoroughly Modern Millie, Barefoot In The Park, The Whisperers* and *Wait Until Dark.*

Wisely, the final nominations and little gold statuettes were awarded fairly equitably, with the exception of *Bonnie and Clyde.* Neither director Arthur Penn, stars Warren Beatty and Faye Dunaway, nor Michael J Pollard won the Oscars for which they'd been nominated, and the team's disappointment was only slightly mollified by the Cinematography prize given to Burnett Guffey and the Supporting Actress award won by Estelle Parsons.

Best Picture award was won by *In The Heat of the Night,* with Rod Steiger collecting a well-deserved Best Actor Oscar as the film's redneck sheriff. Strangely, his co-star Sidney Poitier failed to gain a nomination either for his superlative work in that, or his excellent showing in *Guess Who's Coming To Dinner?*

Steiger's win was at the expense of Beatty, *The Graduate* newcomer Dustin Hoffman, Paul Newman's classy *Cool Hand Luke* and Spencer Tracy's *Guess Who's Coming To Dinner?*

The latter was considered a strong contender, not least because it had proved to be his last screen appearance, but the award of Best Actress award to his long-time sidekick Katharine Hepburn satisfied the Academy's duty to come up with a Pass-The-Kleenex moment. It also made runners-up of Anne Bancroft, Faye Dunaway, Dame Edith Evans (for the spooky *The Whisperers*) and Audrey Hepburn (for the scary *Wait Until Dark*).

The Director prize was won by Mike Nichols, for *The Graduate*, the Supporting Actor award by George Kennedy (for *Cool Hand Luke*), and Estelle Parsons' Supporting Actress Oscar meant disappointment for Carol Channing (*Thoroughly Modern Millie*), Mildred Natwick (*Barefoot In The Park*), Beah Richard (*Guess Who's Coming To Dinner?*) and Katherine Ross (*The Graduate*).

The Dirty Dozen scored with a Supporting Actor

Sidney Poitier and Rod Steiger in the Oscar winning In the Heat Of The Night

nomination for John Cassevetes, but one of the year's biggest box-office hits had to be content with only a Sound Effects Oscar for John Poyner. Similarly, *Camelot* was forced to settle with an Adapted Score prize for Alfred Newman and Ken Darby and a Costume Design award for John Truscott.

As for *Doctor Dolittle*, it had to make do with an Original Song award for Leslie Bricusse (*Talk To The Animals*) and a Visual Effects Oscar for LB Abbott. He'd come up with, among other things the double-headed llama known as The Push-Me-Pull-You.

Oh yes, this year's ceremony was delayed for two days because of Martin Luther King's assassination. Too many members of the Hollywood community wanted to attend his funeral, and the show was not televized until the civil rights leader had been buried.

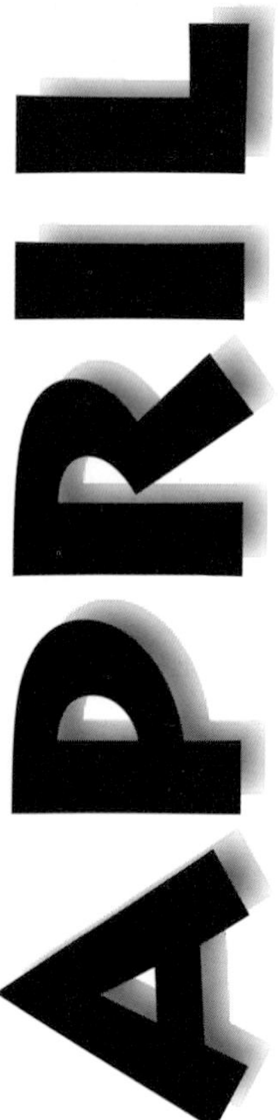

APRIL 8

Success For Sandie

Bare-footed babe Sandie Shaw (pictured) finally ended a frustrating run of British near misses in the Eurovision Song Contest tonight in Vienna when she performed *Puppet On A String.* Written by Tin Pan Alley songsmiths Bill Martin and Phil Coulter, its 'oom-pah' rhythms particularly suited the Austrian venue, and swept the board to give Britain a rare victory.

Although the singer would later describe *Puppet On A String* as 'sexist drivel with a cuckoo-clock tune', it nevertheless attracted the attention of 8.85 million British households and many millions more Europe-wide. The song had already charted before Sandie competed, so sure of victory was her record company – and it stayed at No 1 for three weeks.

APRIL 1

Watch Out Whitehall!

From today, anyone with a complaint about unfair treatment from a British Government department or official body could appeal via his or her MP to the new Ombudsman (Swedish for 'legal representative'). The man who took on the job of dealing with an expected 7,000 complaints each year was Sir Edmund Compton, who fired an immediate warning shot across the bows of the Government and Civil Service when he promised to 'investigate ministries from the minister downwards'. His message was clear, Whitehall had better watch out!

APRIL 19

Germany's 'Greatest Statesman' Dies

KONRAD ADENAUER, the statesman who was widely accepted as having been the architect of West Germany's post-war recovery, prosperity and return to international respectability, died today at his home near Bonn, at the age of 91.

Affectionately known by his allies as 'Der Alte' (the old one), and as 'the old fox' to his enemies and rivals, Adenauer became the first Chancellor of West Germany in 1949, remaining in the post until 1963 when his country's reconstruction was almost complete.

Founder of the Christian Democratic Union party in the mid-1940s, Adenauer worked tirelessly to achieve the reunification of Germany - an ambition which made him the special target of Soviet vilification - and full reconciliation with France and the rest of a Europe the Nazis had done so much to humiliate and destroy during World War II.

After a state funeral in Cologne, Adenauer would be buried in his family's tomb in Rhondorf, the home-town to which he had retired.

APRIL 7

Radio Revolution In San Francisco

Veteran disc jockey and programme controller Tom 'Big Daddy' Donahue chose radio station KMPX in San Francisco as his guinea-pig for 'progressive FM radio', a concept which went 'on-air' for the first time today and which would, in the next few years, change the face of US airwaves.

With the policy of low-key disc jockeys playing mainly album tracks rather than the hit singles of the day, and restricting their on-air chat to a minimum, 'progressive' or 'underground' radio offered a stark contrast to the bubblegum-crazed norm with its incessant jingles and non-musical interruptions.

By making radio hip again, it would offer the new breed of rock bands the oxygen of publicity that helped make the US West Coast in general – and San Francisco in particular – a crucible of musical innovation in the late 1960s.

UK TOP 10 SINGLES

1: Somethin' Stupid
- Nancy and Frank Sinatra

2: Puppet On A String
- Sandie Shaw

3: Release Me
- Engelbert Humperdinck

4: This Is My Song
- Harry Secombe

5: A Little Bit Me, A Little Bit You
- The Monkees

6: Simon Smith & His Amazing Dancing Bear
- The Alan Price Set

7: I Was Kaiser Bill's Batman
- Whistling Jack Smith

8: Ha Ha Said The Clown
- Manfred Mann

9: Edelweiss
- Vince Hill

10: It's All Over
- Cliff Richard

ARRIVALS

Born this month:
5: Erland Johnsen, Norwegian international football player
20: Alan McLoughlin, Republic of Ireland football player
25: Alan Kernaghan, Republic of Ireland football player

DEPARTURES

Died this month:
13: Luis Somoza Debayle, Nicaraguan politician, aged 44
19: Konrad Adenauer, German statesman, Chancellor of the Federal Republic 1949-63 *(see main story)*
29: JB Lenoir, US blues singer, guitarist, aged 38; Anthony Mann, US film director (*The Glenn Miller Story, The Man From Laramie, El Cid,* etc), aged 61

APRIL 21

Greek Colonels Seize Power In Coup

THE PEOPLE OF GREECE found themselves subject to curfew and martial law today following a coup by a right wing group of army officers headed by Colonel George Papadopoulos. Prime Minister George Papandreous was arrested, together with his son who was suspected of a left-wing plot to seize undemocratic control of the country.

Greece's new rulers didn't seem to be content with exerting political influence, for in an unprecedented move they ordered boys to get their hair cut and forbade girls to wear the fashionable new mini-skirt, even banning bearded tourists the following month!

However, the Colonels faced the continuing opposition of King Constantine who, while he officiated at the swearing-in of the new government, refused to sign a decree intended to suspend constitutional freedoms in the country which once prided itself on being the birthplace of democracy.

APRIL 24

Russian Cosmonaut Dies In Mystery Crash

Following the three American astronaut deaths in the *Apollo* mission tragedy earlier this year, the US-Soviet space race claimed another victim today when Soviet cosmonaut Vladimir Komarov crashed to his doom after the parachute on his re-entry capsule malfunctioned.

NASA scientists keenly observing the Soyuz mission believed that the preceding 24-hour mission may also not have gone entirely according to plan, with communications between the spacecraft and Soviet ground control cut off for more than twelve hours and the 40-year-old Komarov's first attempt at re-entering the earth's atmosphere an aborted failure.

APRIL 12

First Hit For Playwright Stoppard

As anticipated by those in the know, the opening night of newcomer Tom Stoppard's play *Rosencrantz And Guildenstern Are Dead* at London's National Theatre was a resounding success, following its run at the Edinburgh Festival and the *London Evening* Standard award that ensued.

The play, loosely based on Shakespeare's characters from *Hamlet*, posed deep philosophical conundrums about the meaninglessness of life, but was served up in a humorous fashion which was to earn Stoppard the reputation of a metaphysical wit whose avowed aim was 'the perfect marriage between the play of ideas and farce'.

APRIL 8

National Pile-Up Gives 100-1 Winner

In scenes reminiscent of the *Charge of the Light Brigade*, a massive tangle of fallen, riderless and halted horses at the 23rd fence of the Grand National steeplechase classic turned the Aintree Racecourse in Liverpool to bedlam today - and allowed a 100-1 outsider to steer his way through the pile-up and race home the winner. The horse was *Foinavon*, his rider was John Buckingham, and Britain's bookmakers probably had a celebratory drink or two as all the heavy money vanished into that tangle on the course.

MAY 1

Elvis Marries Priscilla

TO THE INTENSE disappointment of his female fans who continued to live in the vain hope of somehow becoming Mrs Presley, rock idol Elvis married his long-time sweetheart, Priscilla Beaulieu, in Las Vegas today. Some 14 friends were present at the ceremony itself, and 100 at the champagne breakfast that followed.

Both bride and groom were from Memphis, Tennessee, but rock'n'roll's greatest love affair had started when Sergeant 53310761 Presley, E (as he was known during his two years in the US Army) met the then 14 year old Priscilla in September 1959 in Bad Neuheim, Germany, where her stepfather, a US Air Force captain, was based. Their friendship later deepened to love and Priscilla - heavily chaperoned at all times, it was stressed when word leaked out - moved into the Presley mansion, Graceland, when she was only 16 years old.

In 1968 the couple would have a daughter, Lisa Marie (who in 1994 would herself marry a pop icon, Michael Jackson), but would divorce in October 1973. After initial acrimony, they would resume their friendship and it would be Priscilla - by then an accomplished film and TV actress - who would take charge of sorting out the Presley empire's muddled finances when Elvis died in 1977.

MAY 10

Stones On Drugs Charges

Two members of the controversial rock band, The Rolling Stones - singer Mick Jagger and guitarist Keith Richards - today appeared before Chichester magistrates to answer drugs charges laid against them after police raided Richards' Sussex home on February 12. The two pleaded not guilty and were each granted bail of £1,000.

By coincidence (according to police), the London flat of fellow-Rolling Stone Brian Jones was also raided today, and he too now faced charges of possession.

The much-publicized Jagger-Richards trial in June - which included a great amount of salacious detail about a naked girl wrapped in a fur rug (Jagger's girlfriend, the singer Marianne Faithfull, who was not charged with any offence) - would inspire a *Times* editorial headlined 'Who breaks a butterfly on a wheel?'

That was the outraged reaction of the paper to the sentences given the musicians, Richards got a year and Jagger three months. Both would walk free when an appeal court quashed Keith's sentence entirely and reduced Mick's to a conditional discharge.

When he came to court, Brian Jones would be fined £1,000 after psychiatric evidence of suicidal tendencies blocked a jail term.

MAY 16

De Gaulle Says Conditional 'Non' To Britain

Yet again, French President Charles de Gaulle rejected British efforts to join the Common Market. Although he didn't actually say 'no' today, he indicated that the British Government would have to abandon its so-called 'special relationship' with the United States and begin to act like 'good Europeans' before the UK would be allowed in.

The decision was a severe blow for British pro-marketeers who had recently gained a majority of 488 votes to 62 in the House of Commons, overcoming opposition to Britain's application on both sides of the House. Prime Minister Harold Wilson said that the Government was not giving up, and indeed would continue to press for Britain's membership of the EEC.

Frost Over England

David Frost was British television's man of the moment in 1967, with his Frost Report nudging into the UK TV Top 10 for the first time this month.

The year had begun with him fronting the hard-hitting *Frost Programme* for the London-based Rediffusion channel in London, before he switched to the BBC for *Frost Over England,* for which a humorous touch was injected by the likes of the *Two Ronnies,* Corbett and Barker, and future Monty Python man John Cleese.

To round off a good year, Frost and his business partners then won one of the most high-profile of British independent TV franchises, the result was London Weekend Television, which would start broadcasting in 1968.

UK TOP 10 SINGLES

1: Puppet On A String
- Sandie Shaw

2: Dedicated To The One I Love
- The Mamas & The Papas

3: Somethin' Stupid
- Nancy and Frank Sinatra

4: Silence Is Golden
- The Tremeloes

5: The Boat That I Row
- Lulu

6: Pictures Of Lily
- The Who

7: Funny Familiar Forgotten Feeling
- Tom Jones

8: Purple Haze
- The Jimi Hendrix Experience

9: Seven Drunken Nights
- The Dubliners

10: A Little Bit Me, A Little Bit You
- The Monkees

ARRIVALS

Born this month:
2: David Rocastle, English football player
27: Paul Gascoigne, England international football player

DEPARTURES

Died this month:
12: John Masefield, British Poet Laureate, aged 88
15: Edward Hopper, US painter, aged 84
30: Claude Rains, UK film and stage actor, aged 76 ***(see main story)***
31: Billy Strayhorn, US composer, pianist, long-time collaborator with Duke Ellington, aged 51

MAY 28

Lone Yachtsman Chichester Lands At Plymouth – Late!

HE MIGHT HAVE BEEN ten hours late arriving, but that was clearly of little concern to a man who had just taken seven and a half months to complete an epic 28,500 mile voyage. Certainly, the vast crowd gathered today in Plymouth for the arrival of the first man to sail single-handed around the world - lone yachtsman Sir Francis Chichester - didn't seem to mind the extra wait.

They greeted the popular record-breaker with huge cheers as he received a 'welcome home' message from the Queen and Prince Philip, and from the Prime Minister, Harold Wilson, just as his *Gipsy Moth IV* had received a victory salute from the hundreds of boats which turned out for his arrival at the Royal Western Yacht Club.

Sir Francis, who was also welcomed by his wife and his son, Giles, appeared a little unsteady as he stepped ashore for the congratulations of Plymouth's Lord Mayor. The 65-year-old was then driven through packed streets to the Guildhall, acclaimed as a true hero.

MAY 30

Hollywood Mourns So-Suave Rains

No-one played a suave Englishman quite like Claude Rains, whose death at the age of 78 was announced today. That was because Rains really was a suave Englishman who became one of Hollywood's most successful actors by keeping it simple, incisive and carefully understated.

Rains did not make his screen début until 1933, when his portrayal of *The Invisible Man* set him off on a career which spanned more than 30 years and included such film classics as *The Adventures Of Robin Hood, King's Row, Casablanca, Lawrence Of Arabia* and his final appearance, *The Greatest Story Ever Told.*

Strangely, for a man whose playing often helped transform good films into special or great ones, Rains never received a major acting award.

MAY 25

Celtic Win European Cup

At their first attempt in the competition, Glasgow Celtic today became the first British football team to bring home the European Champions' Cup, beating Inter Milan 2-1 in Lisbon, despite conceding an early penalty. Heroic defensive work for the first hour kept the damage to a minimum, and when full-back Tommy Gemmell equalized with a thunderous shot the Italians were undone. A second goal eight minutes from the final whistle, by Steve Chalmers, wrapped the game up for a team captained superbly by towering defender Billy McNeill and managed inspirationally by Jock Stein.

Appointed in 1965, Stein had fashioned a team that would win the Scottish League ten times (including a world record nine in a row between 1966 and 1974). However, his other visit to the European Cup Final, in 1970, would end in a 2-1 defeat by the Dutch side, Feyenoord.

MAY 30

Biafra Secedes From Nigeria

Today's declaration of independence by Biafra, the eastern region of Nigeria, received a swift reaction from the mother country's leader, Lieutenant Colonel Gowon. He described the secession as treasonous, immediately closed the joint border to trade and simultaneously threatened military retaliation.

While the newly-claimed Republic of Biafra was inhabited mainly by the Christian members of the Ibo tribe, the remainder of Nigeria was governed by Muslims of the Hausa tribe. The declaration marked the beginning of a bitter three-year civil war which was to bring Biafra to its knees and Nigeria to the edge of economic ruin.

JUNE 5

First - And Last - Blood To Israel In Six-Day War

WITH A SHIPPING BLOCKADE ordered by Egypt's President Nasser effectively shutting Israel's only port on the Gulf of Aqaba at Eilat, Israeli forces today took retaliatory action. They struck at Arab airfields to destroy 400 Egyptian, Syrian and Jordanian Air Force planes in the first action of what was accurately described as the 'Six-Day War'.

Although Egyptian forces initially put up stiff opposition to the attack, at the end of the first three days Israeli forces directed by Defence Minister Moshe Dayan were moving deep into the Sinai peninsula, pressing west as far as the Suez Canal and the strategic fortress of Sharm el Sheikh.

Egypt stood defeated and its principal ally, Jordan, had fared no better as Jericho, Bethlehem and Jerusalem all fell to the Israeli advance. Those gains meant that devout Jews were once again able to worship at the holy Wailing Wall in Jerusalem, while the Arab world was in turmoil.

President Nasser accused the United States and Britain of aiding the Israeli attack – charges which were denied - while leading oil-producing Arab states cut off supplies to the West.

On the fifth day, President Nasser tendered his resignation to the Egyptian National Assembly, but was gratified when his gesture was rejected as huge rallies in Cairo and Beirut urged him to stay in office.

On Day 6, with their forces now 12 miles inside Syria and holding Arab territory many times larger than their own country, the Israeli government finally conceded to United Nations calls for a ceasefire. They had scored a major victory. Long-term peace would, the Israelis knew, be harder to win.

JUNE 12

Bach To Basics As Procol Hit Top

Performed by Procol Harum, an unknown group from Southend, England, *A Whiter Shade Of Pale* today began a five-week run at the top of the UK charts. The song, with an organ-based melody highly reminiscent of Bach's *Air On A G String,* featured incomprehensible words from the group's non-performing lyricist Keith Reid, sung by the music writer and pianist Gary Brooker. The band, previously known as The Paramounts, whose new name was similar to the Latin for 'beyond these things', would never progress beyond their début in commercial terms (it also reached No 5 in the US), but the song became one of the sounds of the so-called Summer of Love, along with Scott McKenzie's *San Francisco.*

JUNE 7

Death Dogs Dorothy Parker And Claims Tracy

The US - and the world - lost two of its most potent cultural figures this month with the deaths of the poet and short-story writer, Dorothy Parker, and film actor Spencer Tracy.

Parker, a legendary figure in the New York literary scene, died alone in her Manhattan apartment on June 7, with just her poodle, Troy, present. She was 73 years old.

Born Dorothy Rothschild, her mother's early death, her violent dislike of her stepmother and the convent school to which she was sent, undoubtedly helped to form a personality capable of the most acerbic wit and outstanding satire, all of which she used to devastating effect as an essayist, theatre and literary critic to become acknowledged queen of the New York literary scene in the 1920s and 1930s.

Famous for her many quips ('You can lead a horticulture, but you can't make her think', 'She was the original good time had by all', and 'Men seldom make passes at girls who wear glasses'), she nevertheless managed to disprove the theory that men steer clear of girls with sharp minds, she was married twice and had a string of love affairs.

The death of Spencer Tracy, at the age of 67 on June 10, robbed Hollywood of one of its most accomplished players, whose two Academy Awards did not begin to reflect his skill, nor the immense affection in which he was held by three generations of filmgoers. *(For a full appreciation of Tracy, see Came & Went pages).*

UK TOP 10 SINGLES

1: A Whiter Shade Of Pale
- Procol Harum

2: Silence Is Golden
- The Tremeloes

3: Waterloo Sunset
- The Kinks

4: There Goes My Everything
- Engelbert Humperdinck

5: The Happening
- The Supremes

6: Then I Kissed Her
- The Beach Boys

7: Dedicated To The One I Love
- The Mamas & The Papas

8: Sweet Soul Music
- Arthur Conley

9: Carrie-Ann
- The Hollies

10: The Wind Cries Mary
- The Jimi Hendrix Experience

ARRIVALS

Born this month:

8: Efan Ekoku, Nigerian international football player

18: Alex Bunbury, Canadian international football player

DEPARTURES

Died this month:

3: Arthur Mitchell Ransome, UK children's author (*Swallows And Amazons,* etc), aged 83; Arthur, Lord Tedder, British commander, Marshal of the Royal Air Force, aged 76

8: Laverne Andrews, US singer, of The Andrews Sisters, aged 51

29: Jayne Mansfield (Vera Jane Palmer), US film actress (*The Girl Can't Help It, The Wayward Bus,* etc), aged 35; Primo Carnera, Italian boxer, world heavyweight champion 1933-35, aged 60

Bonnie & Clyde Shoot To Stardom

Based on the real-life careers of bank-robbing couple Clyde Barrow and Bonnie Parker, this summer's movie blockbuster, *Bonnie And Clyde,* was to net far more dollars for its stars, Warren Beatty and Faye Dunaway, than the original duo ever dreamed of stealing.

Set in the 1930s Depression years, the sly combination of comedy and violence which the movie purveyed had already raised many an eyebrow, while the little-known 26-year-old Dunaway - who only got the part of Bonnie when first choices Natalie Wood and Tuesday Weld proved unavailable - looked to have a fine future in front of her.

JUNE 1

Beatles Release Landmark 'Sgt Pepper'

The Beatles began a momentous month, even by their standards, by releasing *Sgt Pepper's Lonely Hearts Club Band,* probably the most impressive of any of their many superb albums and one whose every nuance - from George Martin's multi-layered production, through the controversial cover collage, to Lennon and McCartney's songs - would inspire a generation of rock musicians to a frenzy of experimentation, and a host of music critics to new heights of breathtaking pomposity.

Later, on June 25, The Beatles performed the epic *All You Need Is Love* on the first completely world-wide satellite link-up, to give their new single an unprecedented 'plug' to an audience of several billion.

Neither this, nor their recent double-sided No 1 single *Penny Lane/Strawberry Fields Forever,* were included on the *Sgt Pepper* album, proof that the world's most talented pop group was also among the most prolific.

JUNE 18

Monterey Goes Pop

Today saw the largest collection of rock superstars ever to appear on one bill when 50,000 fans gathered for the Monterey International Pop Festival in California. Even for the state which was the birthplace of flower power, the line-up of hip musicians was formidable, thanks to The Mamas and The Papas' John Phillips, who organized the event with producer Lou Adler, plus Paul McCartney as talent consultant and Rolling Stone Brian Jones helping out as one of the compères.

The concert, which featured the likes of Jefferson Airplane, The Mamas and The Papas, Jimi Hendrix, Janis Joplin, The Who and Indian sitar player Ravi Shankar, was inevitably a sell-out, declaring that the age of the rock festival had well and truly begun. It also made an overnight pop star of the soul singer Otis Redding.

Film-maker DA Pennebaker immortalized the event for good measure as the documentary *Monterey Pop.*

JUNE 28

Death Toll Mounts In US Race Riots

IN A YEAR IN WHICH civil rights marches vied with anti-war protests for public attention in the US, June was no exception. Feelings in minority communities were running high and today no fewer than 14 people were reported to have been shot during two days of race riots in Buffalo, New York.

The month of May had seen the National Guard ordered into Mississippi, while in Texas, a policeman was shot dead during a riot on the campus of Texas Southern University. In an attempt to curb racist legislation, on June 12 the US Supreme Court had ruled that individual states could not lawfully ban interracial marriages.

By July, the summer of discontent would reach epidemic proportions and President Johnson would be forced to set up a special commission to investigate the causes of the race riots which were, by then, spread across the nation. In Detroit, where 38 died, 4,700 paratroopers would be mobilized to deal with wholescale looting.

ALL-CONQUERING CELTIC BRING EUROPEAN CUP HOME

With the tactical genius Jock Stein in the manager's chair and team captain Billy 'Caesar' McNeill marshalling his troops brilliantly during matches to justify his nickname, Glasgow Celtic were in the middle of an unprecedented roll this year which would see them top a clean sweep of the Scottish trophy cabinet by becoming the first British soccer club to win the European Cup.

In Lisbon, in front of a 55,000 crowd, Celtic finally broke the hoodoo which had limited British involvement in the previous eleven finals to providing the venue - Glasgow in 1960, when 127,000 fans had witnessed Real Madrid's astonishing 7-3 victory over Eintracht Frankfurt, and Wembley in 1963 when a disappointing 45,000 had seen Milan beat Benfica 2-1.

Celtic weren't, of course, unbeatable during this period, but they were in the habit of winning so often that they would win the Scottish First Division championship every year from the 1964-65 season until 1973-74, keep a hold on the Scottish League Cup from 1965 to 1969, and this year revenge their 1-0 defeat by Rangers in a re-played 1966 FA Cup final by putting two unanswered goals past Aberdeen.

Internazionale were an entirely different challenge, of course. One of Italy's top teams for the past decade, they'd won the European Cup before, in Vienna in 1964, when 'Sandro' Mazzola scored two of the three goals which beat the mighty Real Madrid. Mazzola was still the sharp point of Inter's rapier-like attack, as he continued to prove in the Italian league and by scoring the goal by which Inter had beaten Benfica to win the 1965 World Club Cup.

His deadly accuracy was proved when he struck to give Internazionale the lead. That ended when the big, sometimes clumsy, but remarkably prolific Tommy Gemmell - a 1960s rarity, a goal-scoring full-back - levelled the score and set the stage for Celtic's centre-forward, Steve Chalmers, to register one of the most memorable victories in his team's long and distinguished history.

LAVER PREPARES TO RECLAIM WORLD TENNIS CROWN

After languishing for five years as a professional banned from the world's great tennis championships, Rod Laver had every reason to welcome the All England Club's decision to bow to the inevitable and make the 1968 Wimbledon tournament open to all players, amateur and professional. Laver had been exiled from the main world events since turning pro shortly after his 1962 Grand Slam season. His absence from the circuit was a tragedy for him, and the game in which he had reigned supreme.

With the Wimbledon blazers - arguably the most conservative sports body in the world - voting to face reality, it could only be a matter of time before the other Grand Slam events, Laver's native Australia, the United States and France, followed suit.

And so it would prove. When the brilliant left-hander returned to fold in 1968, he would reclaim the Wimbledon crown he'd been forced to abdicate in 1962 - the year he'd not only won the four Grand Slam events, but had emerged victorious in the Italian and German championships and won every major tournament he'd entered, including nine major doubles titles, three mixed and six men's.

The prospect of Laver's imminent return was a mouthwatering one for the world's tennis fans. A graceful and agile player, he combined a heavy top-spin attack with a delicate touch close to the net. Arguably the finest player of all time, but unarguably the best player of his generation, Rod Laver was on his way back!

SIMPSON DRUG DEATH SHOCKS CYCLING WORLD

The collapse and death of British road cyclist Tommy Simpson - on July 23 as he and other Tour de France competitors toiled up Mont Ventoux in broiling heat - not only stunned the professional cycling fraternity but led directly to the ban which many international sports bodies would place on a number of drugs. An autopsy revealed that the 29-year-old Simpson had been dosed with stimulants.

Although the use of performance-enhancing substances was widespread (and legal) at the time, especially for endurance events like the Tour, Simpson's death was a tragic warning of the risks they posed for even the fittest of athletes - which he most definitely was, and had proved on many occasions.

Born in County Durham, Simpson had turned professional in 1960 after a distinguished amateur career which had netted him an Olympic bronze in the 1956 team pursuit and a 1958 Commonwealth Games silver in the individual pursuit. More a one-day specialist than a noted tour performer, he had nevertheless become the first Briton to wear the Tour de France's famous leader's yellow jersey in 1962 - if only for a day. He was in overall seventh place when he died.

The French classic had subjected Simpson to severe injury in the past, when he was so badly hurt in a fall that doctors considered amputating an arm. He had survived that to win the 1965 Tour of Lombardy and that year's professional road race championship, victories which - along with wins in the 1961 Tour of Flanders, the 1963 Bordeaux to Paris event, the Milan to San Remo in 1964 and the 1964 Paris-Nice race in the same year - established him as the first great road professional Britain had produced.

Billy McNeill receives the European Cup after the 2-1 victory over Inter Milan

JULY 16

Europeans Flee As Biafra Explodes

With Nigerian troops driving deep into the country's breakaway region of Biafra, thousands of British, European and American nationals were reported fleeing the area today, their escapes often made more hazardous by rebel roadblocks and official government restrictions on civilian movement.

Federal leader General Gowon was using heavy artillery, supported by infantry, to achieve his successes, but at immense cost to the population and to his forces as the rebels scored their own victories.

Most of the area still held by the Biafran forces of Colonel Ojukwu was Nigeria's most important oil-producing region, and he was said to be insisting that British oil companies operating local concessions must pay him the royalties due to the Federal government. Shell-BP was said to be cooperating - about 10 per cent of Britain's oil came from Nigerian wells.

JULY 8

Tragic Beauty Vivien Leigh Dies

VIVIEN LEIGH, (pictured with Laurence Olivier) the English stage and screen beauty who once captivated millions as the wilful Southern belle Scarlett O'Hara in *Gone With The Wind,* and held Broadway and London West End audiences enthralled in classical roles, died today of tuberculosis at the age of 53.

Leigh, who made her name in the mid-1930s with a string of acclaimed stage appearances and a number of notable films, established her star status in 1937 when she played Ophelia to Laurence Olivier's Hamlet. Spotted by Hollywood, she won the part of Scarlett O'Hara in the face of incredible competition from many top-ranked US actresses, and proved producer David Selznick right when she was awarded the first of her two Academy Awards as Best Actress.

Her affair with Laurence Olivier became marriage in 1940, after which the couple were the undisputed royal family of British theatre. Always frail, Leigh began to focus her energies on the periods she and Olivier worked together, and when a series of mental breakdowns occurred, Olivier was unable to cope and ended their marriage. In 1951 Leigh picked up on the southern connection to win her second Oscar as Blanche du Bois in the film version of Tennessee Williams' *A Streetcar Named Desire.*

Although she would continue to work in fits and starts, Vivien Leigh could not maintain her physical and mental strengths long enough for the last decade of her ultimately tragic life to be called a career.

JULY 16

5,000 March To Legalize Pot

London's Hyde Park was the location chosen by organizers of today's 'Legalize Pot 1967' rally which drew the support of more than 5,000 who favoured unfettered access to the happy herb. An emblem of the hippy subculture, the marijuana joint had increasingly become the most favoured means of 'turning on', and many believed its use should be decriminalized.

Only five days earlier, the very proper English prima ballerina, Dame Margot Fonteyn, and her long-time dance partner Rudolf Nureyev had been arrested, along with 16 others, in a police raid on a party in San Francisco. But although marijuana was found on the premises, police said they wouldn't be pressing charges.

It all spelled the end of civilization as they knew it for all those who thought the permissive society had gone too far. Their concern appeared justified in Britain this month with the passage of two Bills through the House of Commons.

UK TOP 10 SINGLES

1: A Whiter Shade Of Pale
- Procol Harum

2: Alternate Title
- The Monkees

3: There Goes My Everything
- Engelbert Humperdinck

4: She'd Rather Be With Me
- The Turtles

5: It Must Be Him (Seul Sur Son Étoile)
- Vikki Carr

6: All You Need Is Love
- The Beatles

7: Carrie-Ann
- The Hollies

8: See Emily Play
- Pink Floyd

9: If I Were A Rich Man
- Topol

10: San Francisco (Be Sure To Wear Some Flowers In Your Hair)
- Scott McKenzie

JULY 3

'News At Ten' Is Launched

Britain's Independent Television (ITV) made its own mark when it launched a new late-night news programme tonight. Designed to provide a half-hour round-up of the day's main events, *News At Ten* was set to rival the BBC's *Nine O'Clock News.* With its imposing signature tune featuring the chimes of Big Ben and a catalogue of stalwart newsreaders, it soon became a British broadcasting institution and survived into the 1990s in some style.

ARRIVALS

Born this month:

1: **Pamela Anderson, US TV actress (Baywatch)**

DEPARTURES

Died this month:

8: **Vivien Leigh (Vivien Hartley), UK film and stage actress, aged 54** ***(see main story)***

17: **John Coltrane, US jazz saxophonist, aged 41** ***(see Came & Went pages)***

21: **Albert Luthuli, South African civil rights leader, Zulu chief, 1960 Nobel Peace Prize winner, aged 69** ***(see Came and Went pages)*****;** **Basil Rathbone, UK stage and film actor, definitive Sherlock Holmes (*****David Copperfield, The Adventures Of Sherlock Holmes, The Hound Of The Baskervilles, Spider Woman,*** **etc), aged 75**

23: **Tommy Simpson, UK champion cyclist** ***(see Sport pages)***

25: **Tommy Duncan, US western swing singer, songwriter with bandleader Bob Wills (*****Take Me Back To Tulsa, Stay A Little Longer,*** **etc)**

JULY 30

De Gaulle Gives Hope To Quebec Separatists

NEVER A SHRINKING VIOLET, the indomitable Charles de Gaulle was also never one to turn down the chance of doing his bit to support Frenchmen outside France, even if it meant inflaming an already volatile situation or causing his official hosts the most severe embarrassment.

Which is exactly what the French President did during his recent visit to Canada when he rallied support for Quebec separatists in Montreal by declaring 'Long live free Quebec!' The 1960s had seen growing demands for Quebec to be allowed to secede from the rest of Canada, and suffered increased violence when those demands had been denied.

De Gaulle had compounded the damage after his rabble-rousing speech when he met Quebec Premier Daniel Johnson but failed to keep an appointment with the Federal Premier, Lester Pearson, after Pearson announced that the idea of a free Quebec was 'unacceptable'.

Back in France today, where his remarks had caused nearly as much debate as they had in Canada, de Gaulle didn't let the matter rest. Throwing another stick of dynamite on the flames, he described Quebec as having suffered, 'a century of oppression which followed the British conquest'.

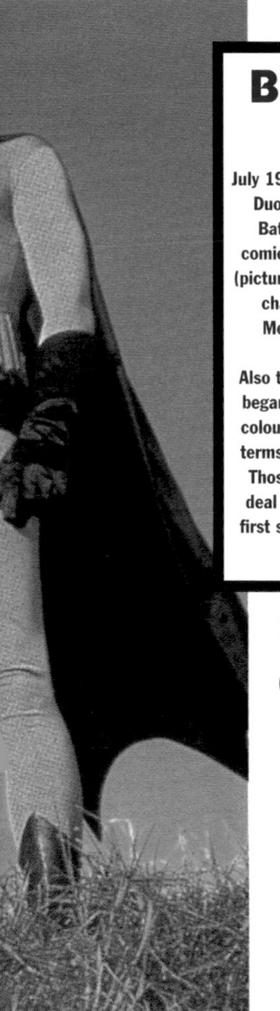

Batman Bursts Onto TV Screens

July 1967 was the month which saw the arrival of the 'Dynamic Duo' on TV screens around the world. Arch crime-fighters Batman and Robin - already famous through best-selling comics - appeared in the guise of Adam West and Burt Ward (pictured), socking it to a selection of baddies including famed character actors Cesar Romero (as The Joker), Burgess Meredith (The Penguin), Julie Newmar (Catwoman) and impressionist Frank Gorshin (The Riddler).

Also this month, Britain's second state-run TV channel, BBC2, began broadcasting in colour, even though the cost of a new colour set was £200 (equivalent to around £1,400 in today's terms) and the UK television licence fee was doubled to £10. Those well-heeled enough to indulge were treated to a good deal of green and white on the new channel's first day - the first six hours or so were devoted almost entirely to coverage of the Wimbledon Tennis Championships!

Raquel Struts Her (Jurassic) Stuff

Having been shot to fame – literally – in the 1966 sci-fi epic *Fantastic Voyage,* which saw her miniaturized and injected into a man's body, statuesque starlet Raquel Welch was again setting male pulses racing in her new movie, *One Million Years BC.* The dialogue for this piece of amiable nonsense consisted of little more than grunts – but Raquel strode among the cavemen in her animal-skin two-piece as if to the manner born.

Married and divorced by 21, with two children, ravishing Raquel – the sex symbol of 1967 – seemed here to stay.

JULY 20

Return Of The Killer

Rock'n'roll piano-pumping legend Jerry Lee Lewis returned to Britain today for the first time since 1958, when his marriage to his 14-year-old third cousin Myra was first disclosed. Then the hellraiser known as 'The Killer' had been booed from the stage, denounced from newspaper leader columns and found his tour curtailed. But this time round people seemed happy to forgive and forget.

Lewis's shows would be well attended and well-received – almost too much so. While performing at the Sunbury Jazz and Blues Festival in August his show was interrupted when officials asked him to leave the stage, saying he'd driven his audience into an apparently uncontrollable frenzy!

AUGUST 27

Mystery Death Of Beatles Manager Epstein

THE RECORD INDUSTRY was stunned today to hear of the death of the world's most celebrated manager, Brian Epstein (pictured), the 32-year-old who discovered The Beatles in Liverpool's Cavern club and masterminded their rise to superstar status. Epstein's body was found by his butler in a locked bedroom in his London home, an apparent victim of a sleeping pills overdose.

The Beatles, who were communing with their spiritual mentor, the Maharishi Mahesh Yogi, at Bangor University, North Wales, broke off their planned five-day meditation course and rushed to London on hearing the news. A visibly shocked John Lennon told reporters, 'I don't know where we would have been without Brian'.

Epstein's death was, by any standards, a mysterious one and would remain a mystery despite exhaustive police enquiries and the increasingly wild theories of tabloid journalists. He was homosexual, and while that was an open secret in music business circles, it has been suggested that he'd been threatened with 'outing' at a time when homosexuality was still widely viewed as far beyond the pale. He was also known to have been distressed at what he perceived as a growing distance between him and The Beatles.

Disregarding how the group must have felt, the Maharishi reportedly deemed Epstein's death 'not important', being merely part of the physical world and not the spiritual.

AUGUST 1

Black Leader Calls For Armed Violence

Continued resistance from some quarters of the US establishment was turning some black leaders against the concept of non-violent demonstration as a means of securing wider civil rights for their communities.

This was evidenced most dramatically today when Stokely Carmichael, previously Chairman of the Student Non-violent Co-ordinating Committee, announced that 'We have no alternative but to use aggressive armed violence in order to own the land, houses and stores inside our communities, and to control the politics of those communities'.

Change was coming, but obviously not quickly enough for a growing number of militants.

AUGUST 9

Final Curtain For Controversial Orton

British playwright Joe Orton, who achieved as much notoriety as acclaim for his outrageous plays *Entertaining Mr Sloane* and *Loot,* became the subject of even more headlines today when he was murdered by his lover, the artist Kenneth Halliwell. Orton, who was 34, delighted in the scandalized reaction his work provoked which, while often extremely funny, emphasized the corruption, perversions and apparent degeneracy of the 1960s generation.

On September 4 the London inquest into Orton's death would hear that the Leicester-born writer had been victim of a frenzied attack by Halliwell, a man witnesses said had been increasingly jealous of Orton's fame and success. Halliwell then committed suicide.

AUGUST 17

The Chin Changes Channels

Jimmy Hill, the former player who'd turned manager to steer Coventry Football Club from English Third Division obscurity to a place in the First Division in only five years, today announced his resignation and a move to a career as a game summarizer with London Weekend Television.

Hill, who had also been chairman of the players' union, the PFA, would continue to peddle his outspoken opinions, latterly with the BBC. After a less successful spell as managing director of Coventry from 1975-83, he would return to Fulham FC - the club with which he'd had most success as a player - to become its chairman and help save it from extinction.

UK TOP 10 SINGLES

1: San Francisco (Be Sure To Wear Some Flowers In Your Hair)
- Scott McKenzie

2: All You Need Is Love
- The Beatles

3: I'll Never Fall In Love Again
- Tom Jones

4: Death Of A Clown
- Dave Davies

5: I Was Made To Love Her
- Stevie Wonder

6: It Must Be Him (Seul Sur Son Étoile)
- Vikki Carr

7: Up Up And Away
- The Johnny Mann Singers

8: Just Loving You
- Anita Harris

9: She'd Rather Be With Me
- The Turtles

10: Even The Bad Times Are Good
- The Tremeloes

ARRIVALS

Born this month:

10: Lorraine Pearson, UK pop singer (5 Star)

15: MCA (Adam Yauch), US rap/pop star (The Beastie Boys)

DEPARTURES

Died this month:

1: Siegfried Sassoon, UK poet, aged 80

9: Anton Walbrook (Adolf Wohlbruck), German-born UK film actor (*The Red Shoes, La Ronde*), aged 67; Joe Orton, British playwright, aged 34 *(see main story)*

13: Jane Darwell (Patti Woodward), US Academy Award winning film actress (*The Grapes Of Wrath, Mary Poppins*), aged 87

15: René Magritte, Belgian surrealist painter *(see main story)*

25: Paul Muni (Muni Weisenfreund), Austrian-American stage and Acadamy Award winning film actor (*Scarface, The Life Of Emile Zola*, etc), aged 71

27: Brian Epstein, British manager of The Beatles, aged 32 *(see main story)*

AUGUST 14

Radio Pirates Sign Off - Bar One!

With the British government's Marine Broadcasting Act due to became law the next day - after which they, their studios, equipment and assets could be seized and impounded while all owners and staff could be prosecuted - most of Britain's so-called 'pirate' radio stations signed off today.

All except one, that is. *Radio Caroline* (pictured), the station which started it all in 1964 when it started broadcasting non-stop rock music from a ship moored outside British territorial waters, was determined to continue.

Despite shipwrecks, boarding parties and various other inconveniences, *Caroline* would carry on ruling the (air)waves until the early 1990s.

AUGUST 30

London Street Fight Deepens UK-Chinese Rift

THE LATEST EXCHANGE in an ongoing and increasingly violent tit-for-tat diplomatic battle between Britain and China left one policeman and one Chinese diplomat injured in London, the British Consulate in Beijing sacked by Red Guards, and the house of the British Chargé d'Affairs looted.

Events in China had led to the British government imposing travel restrictions on Chinese diplomats in London. This was clearly viewed poorly by the staff of the Chinese Mission and they decided to act today.

With police parked outside the Mission to keep watch on the diplomats' movements, a group of Chinese emerged from the building carrying axes, baseball bats and iron bars, launching themselves at officers in full view of watching journalists.

The police were forced to defend themselves with handy dustbin lids in what British Foreign Office officials described as 'deplorable incidents' which were viewed as an attempt by the Chinese to discredit British security forces by drawing them into a fight.

AUGUST 15

Magritte's Brush With Mortality

René Magritte, the Belgian surrealist painter who died today, tried hard to describe the nature of art in his paintings, but only succeeded in deepening the mystery for most. Many of his works challenged the laws of nature in a way that puzzled those who viewed them, but for Magritte the impossibility of what he depicted was the very point of his art, they were just paintings, nothing more. None illustrated this view better than his picture of a tobacco pipe with the caption 'This is not a pipe'. Naturally it wasn't a pipe, it was a painting. Magritte's images had a dream-like quality which was more serene than many of the nightmares depicted by some of his fellow surrealists.

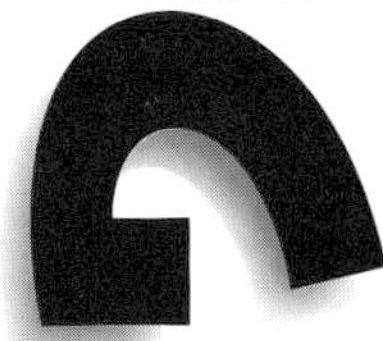

AUGUST 12

Mac Attack Hits Windsor...Minus One

Fleetwood Mac, the British blues band that became an international success story and soap opera in the 1970s, made their first public appearance today at the Windsor Jazz and Blues Festival.

Alongside lead guitarist Peter Green, drummer Mick Fleetwood and second guitarist Jeremy Spencer, stood an unknown figure – bass player Bob Brunning, recruited from a *Melody Maker* advertisement since first-choice John McVie had opted to stay in the comparatively secure employ of bandleader John Mayall.

McVie would relent soon after, however, displacing Brunning who re-entered teaching and rose to headmaster status. Fleetwood Mac, with only Mick Fleetwood still on board from that Windsor début, play on in the 1990s, having meanwhile released *Rumours,* the second biggest-selling rock album ever, in 1977.

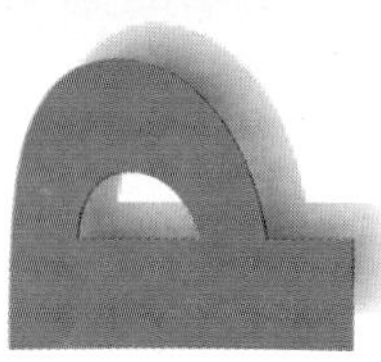

Jimi Hendrix - The Shy Revolutionary

Even by the freaky standards of the psychedelic movement which typified much of the 1967 rock music scene worldwide, Jimi Hendrix was exceptionally freaky - both to look at and to hear. But this year he was destined to burst from complete obscurity, rocket to outstanding recording success, and become the most unmissable act on the world concert and festival circuit.

Born James Marshall Hendrix, in Seattle, in 1942, Hendrix had spent his formative years playing blues and working as a backing musician for a variety of top US soul and rock'n'roll acts, including Little Richard, BB King, The Isley Brothers and Ike and Tina Turner. In 1966 he was based with a band in New York's 'Café Wha' when he was 'discovered' by Chas Chandler, former bassist with top British group The Animals but now embarking on a management career.

Unable to believe that no one else saw the potential in Hendrix that he did, Chandler persuaded Jimi to move to London where he put him together with bassist Noel Redding and drummer Mitch Mitchell. The Jimi Hendrix Experience was born, and when they finally played a few showcase dates in select London clubs where the current rock elite (Beatles, Stones, The Who included) hung out, Chandler's hunch was proved right.

Within days, Jimi's public relations campaign was being handled, free of charge, by the likes of Paul McCartney and Mick Jagger who'd push Jimi's name into every conversation they had with journalists, while Eric Clapton - arguably Britain's undisputed guitar king - let it be known that Jimi Hendrix was a genius in the process of redefining the art of rock guitar.

Signed to The Who's Track Records label, The Jimi Hendrix Experience was launched in January this year via the single *Hey Joe,* which was only the first of four to become UK and European Top 10 hits (the others being *Purple Haze, The Wind Cries Mary* and *Burning Of The Midnight Lamp*). But it was the Hendrix stage show which made him a genuine major star.

Fans who packed every club and hall Hendrix and Co played did so unsure what they'd witness that night. Would Jimi set fire to his guitar? Would he smash it up? Would he play it with his teeth, or behind his head? Would he saw it up and down his microphone stand to pull strangled moans from the strings?

By the end of the year, thanks to Paul McCartney's insistence that he be added to the line-up of the Monterey Pop Festival in California, Jimi Hendrix was a sensation in the US too. And, while The Jimi Hendrix Experience would only record three albums before breaking up in late 1968, and Jimi himself would be dead by the end of 1970, what he began in 1967 was destined to live on and on as subsequent generations discovered his music and couldn't believe what they were hearing.

BAD VIBES AS BEACH BOYS BATTLE THROUGH '67

Having replaced The Beatles as British fans' favourite group in the 1966 *New Musical Express* poll, and their revolutionary 1966 *Pet Sounds* album having been an admitted influence, challenge and spur to The Beatles as they set out to record their 1967 album *Sgt Pepper's Lonely Hearts Club Band,* The Beach Boys could have consolidated their newfound superiority this year. Instead, much of their energy was spent in litigation and confusion.

With leader Brian Wilson (retired from live work with nervous stress, but still the songwriting and production powerhouse) working on tracks for a follow-up to *Pet Sounds,* they began by suing Capitol Records for alleged non-payment of royalties - not a move calculated to help the promotion of their releases during the year.

In March drummer Carl Wilson was arrested on draft-dodging charges when he claimed to be a conscientious objector to the Vietnam War. That affair dragged on through various courts, and forced the group to back out of the Monterey Pop Festival in June. Their place was taken by Otis Redding who, along with Jimi Hendrix and Janis Joplin, used his 40 minutes to achieve international stardom.

With Carl acquitted of all charges, but the new album sessions having fallen apart amid the chaos which increased drug use inevitably causes, The Beach Boys formed their own company, Brother Records, in September, coming to a distribution deal with Capitol to help reconcile the royalties business. Only one brand-new release would appear on Brother this year - the wonderful *Good Vibrations* - to hint at what might have been if the Californian quintet had been able to keep their act together.

Jimi Hendrix

SEPTEMBER 4

Street's Queen In TV's Own Royal Wedding

MORE THAN TWELVE MILLION British TV viewers were glued to their screens this evening as the Wedding of the Year unfolded. No, it wasn't royalty tying the knot, but Elsie Tanner (pictured), acknowledged 'queen' of the country's longest-running and most successful 'soap', *Coronation Street*.

Elsie, who was played by actress Patricia Phoenix, was at long last to wed Master Sergeant Steve Tanner, her wartime American sweetheart. The preparations, ceremony and honeymoon took up most of this week's two half-hour episodes, both written by leading playwright Jack Rosenthal.

Viewers were encouraged to buy a *TV Times* special edition, priced at one shilling, to commemorate the event. It probably lasted longer, as a treasured collectors' item, than the Tanner marriage itself. That would be over within a year.

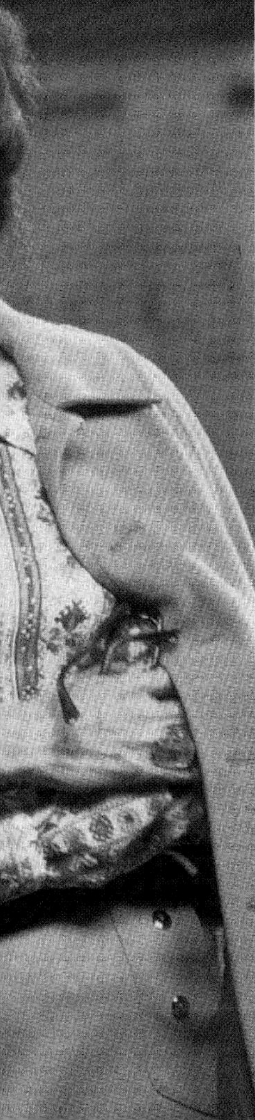

SEPTEMBER 2

Beast Of Buchenwald Found Dead

Ilse Koch, wife of the commandant of the Nazis' Buchenwald death camp, was found hanged with a bedsheet in her West German prison cell today, having decided against serving a life sentence for war crimes.

Even by Nazi standards, Koch's treatment of prison camp inmates was bizarre and cruel. The woman who became known as the 'Beast of Buchenwald' was originally investigated by the Nazi SS in 1943 following reports of systematic torture and lampshades made from the skins of those who had died.

She was subsequently arrested and tried by West Germany and the United States.

SEPTEMBER 30

BBC Plugs Pirate Radio Gap

Keeping its promise to give British teenagers a new service to replace the outlawed pirate radio stations, the BBC today launched Radio 1, its national pop radio channel.

Employing no fewer than 17 ex-pirate disc jockeys - including Kenny Everett, John Peel and Radio Caroline star Tony Blackburn, who played the first record - Radio 1 headed a network from which the old Light, Third and Home Services had disappeared forever, transformed respectively into Radios 2, 3 and 4.

UK TOP 10 SINGLES

1: The Last Waltz
- Engelbert Humperdinck

2: I'll Never Fall In Love Again
- Tom Jones

3: San Francisco (Be Sure To Wear Some Flowers In Your Hair)
- Scott McKenzie

4: Excerpt From A Teenage Opera
- Keith West

5: Itchycoo Park
- The Small Faces

6: Even The Bad Times Are Good
- The Tremeloes

7: Let's Go To San Francisco
- The Flowerpot Men

8: We Love You/Dandelion
- The Rolling Stones

9: Just Loving You
- Anita Harris

10: Heroes And Villains
- The Beach Boys

ARRIVALS

Born this month:

11: Harry Connick Jr, US singer, pianist

18: Ricky Bell, US pop star (New Edition)

20: Ian Carter, Canadian football player; Craig Forrest, Canadian football player

29: Brett Anderson, UK pop star, songwriter (Suede)

DEPARTURES

Died this month:

14: The Earl of Iveagh, Irish brewer, head of Guinness family, aged 83

18: Sir John Douglas Cockcroft, UK nuclear physicist (with Ernest Walton, first to split atom in 1932, first Director of British Atomic Energy Research Establishment, 1951 Nobel Prize for Physics winner), aged 70

29: Carson McCullers, US novelist (*Reflections In A Golden Eye, The Heart Is A Lonely Hunter,* etc), aged 50

SEPTEMBER 9

Waltz In A Name?

Engelbert Humperdinck - real name Arnold George (Gerry) Dorsey, hit No 1 in Britain this month with *The Last Waltz,* his second chart-topper of the year after *Release Me.*

After winning a Belgian song festival, Engelbert had got his big break back home when he deputized for Dickie Valentine on British TV's major variety showcase, *Sunday Night At The London Palladium,* early in 1967. The success of *Release Me* followed, but *The Last Waltz* - written by Les Reed and Barry Mason - would eclipse it, and for years after would provide a suitable close for every disco and church-hall dance in the country.

Newly voted Britain's Show Business Personality of the Year, Engelbert would soon be given his own prime-time TV series, and though the American cabaret circuit beckoned in the 1970s, he would continue his recording career with success into the 1990s.

SEPTEMBER 20

Queen Launches Cunard's New Queen

TODAY WAS A DAY OF celebration on the River Clyde at Glasgow when the new flagship of the Cunard shipping line was launched by the Queen (pictured). A crowd of 100,000 watched and cheered as she named the 58,000 ton passenger liner *Queen Elizabeth II* – or *QE2* for short – and launched her namesake with the traditional champagne bottle.

The job of fitting the ship out for her future work could now begin - it was expected to take 14 months and would provide employment for upwards of 2,000 skilled Clydebank workers.

Hailed as a triumph of British design and engineering when she first entered service across the Atlantic, the *QE2* would sail on into the 1990s as a luxury cruise ship, though a 1994 refit would prove controversial when it was carried out in Germany. In a sad sign of the times, Britain no longer had a shipyard capable of carrying out the work.

SEPTEMBER 25

European Airbus Deal Agreed

A new future for air travel became reality today when Britain, France and West Germany signed an agreement to co-operate in the building of a new *European Airbus* airliner. The twin-engined A300's wide-bodied design was less ambitious than the soon-to-be-flown supersonic *Concorde*, being built by France and Britain.

Different parts of the A300 would be manufactured in the three countries by Aérospatiale, Fokker-VFW and Hawker Siddeley, with the final assembly taking place at Toulouse, in France.

The *Airbus*, which incorporated advanced computer technology to aid its pilots, would prove Europe's biggest challenge to the US domination of the passenger airliner industry by Boeing and Douglas, and many variants - including a four-engined version - would be in service around the world by the 1990s.

SEPTEMBER 10

Gibraltar Vote Confirms UK Links

When the question of unity with Spain was put to the people of Gibraltar today in a long-promised referendum, only 44 out of a population of over 12,000 voted in favour. The people clearly wished to remain under British control.

Spanish claims to the British colony had increased during the past few years and although it was small – only two and a third square miles – it remained strategically important, controlling the narrow Strait of Gibraltar, the only natural entrance to the Mediterranean.

British officials now expected Spain to shut the border forcing travellers to arrive and leave by air.

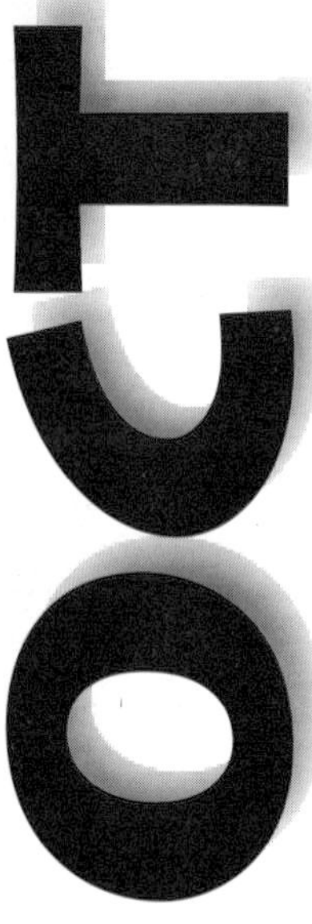

OCTOBER 16

Celebrities Arrested In Anti-war Protests

Anti-Vietnam War rallies reached gigantic proportions in the US this month, with a fair amount of news coverage being given to some of the more famous protesters arrested in the process. First to gain that kind of attention was folk singer and political activist Joan Baez, arrested today in Oakland, California.

A peaceful demonstration at the Selective Service Center, where draftees were processed, was marked by the burning or handing back of draft cards. Draft dodgers were supported by the singing of Miss Baez, who was later arrested for disturbing the peace.

Five days later, a crowd of 50,000 rallied outside the Pentagon in Washington in a demonstration (pictured) which erupted into violence when the crowd stormed lines of soldiers defending the US military headquarters. Among those arrested was the novelist Norman Mailer and rally organizer David Dellinger.

OCTOBER 8

Farewell To Attlee, Creator Of UK's Welfare State

BRITISH SOCIALISTS were in mourning today when Clement Attlee, the man who oversaw the country's momentous post-war welfare reforms, died at the age of 84. Born to a middle-class family in Putney, South London, Attlee was converted to socialism after working as a volunteer in the capital's slums at the beginning of the century.

A barrister by profession, Attlee lectured at the London School of Economics and entered Parliament in 1922, becoming leader of the Labour Party in 1935. He served in Churchill's coalition cabinet during World War II, acting as his Deputy from 1942 to 1945, but it was Labour's post-war landslide election victory which created the opportunity for his far-reaching reforms.

Mining, aviation, broadcasting, railways, road transport, steel and the Bank of England were all nationalized, and the National Health Service - free medical treatment for all - was created. It would prove Attlee's most valuable and enduring legacy.

OCTOBER 29

Hair Today, Hits Tomorrow

***Hair,* the play that would, with its mixture of songs, slogans and nudity, come to embody the essence of the Sixties counterculture, opened tonight at the Public Theatre in New York's East Village. Adapted from a book by Gerome Ragni and James Rado, with music by Galt MacDermot, it told the story of an Oklahoman on his way to enlist in the armed forces to fight in Vietnam who falls in with the 'flower people'. The popular show eventually started a four-year Broadway run and spawned songs that provided hits for The Fifth Dimension (*Aquarius/Let The Sunshine In*), The Cowsills (*Hair*) and Oliver (*Good Morning Starshine*) and a London production.**

OCTOBER 3

Woody Sings His Last Chorus

The influential folk singer and political activist Woody Guthrie died in New York today after a 13-year battle against the wasting disease, Huntington's Chorea. He was only 55 years old.

Born Woodrow Wilson Guthrie, the man who wrote such classics as *This Land Is Your Land* first took to the road in Oklahoma at the age of 15, embarking on a minstrel's life dominated by a concern for others.

Singing in labour union halls and work camps, he supported striking tenant farmers and immigrant workers, and wrote articles as well as songs in support of the downtrodden during the years of the Great Depression.

Guthrie was also the single most important influence on a young folk musician who would prove every bit as radical and influential as his hero. His name? Bob Dylan.

UK TOP 10 SINGLES

1: Massachusetts
- The Bee Gees

2: The Last Waltz
- Engelbert Humperdinck

3: Hole In My Shoe
- Traffic

4: Flowers In The Rain
- The Move

5: The Letter
- The Box Tops

6: Excerpt From A Teenage Opera
- Keith West

7: Reflections
- Diana Ross & The Supremes

8: There Must Be A Way
- Frankie Vaughan

9: Homburg
- Procol Harum

10: Itchycoo Park
- The Small Faces

ARRIVALS

Born this month:
18: Tony Daley, UK football player
20: Susan Tully, UK television actress (*EastEnders*)
21: Paul Ince, England international football player
28: Julia Roberts, US film actress, Oscar nominee (*Pretty Woman, Sleeping With The Enemy,* etc)
30: David White, UK football player

DEPARTURES

Died this month:
3: Woody Guthrie (Woodrow Wilson Guthrie), US folk singer, songwriter, aged 55
8: Clement Richard Attlee, first Earl Attlee, UK statesman, Prime Minister 1945-51 *(see main story)*, aged 80
9: Andre Maurois, French writer, aged 82; Ernesto 'Che' Guevara, Argentinian-Cuban revolutionary *(see main story)*, aged 39
17: Pu Yi, last Emperor of China, aged 61

OCTOBER 31

Queen Mary Leaves For Long Beach

The venerable ocean liner *Queen Mary*, flagship of the Cunard Steamship Company when she made her first Atlantic crossing in 1936, left Southampton for the last time today, destined for Long Beach in California, where the city's council proposed turning her into a floating hotel and conference centre.

The *Queen Mary* served as a glamorous passenger liner in peacetime and, when World War II broke out, was refitted as a troopship. She was able to evade German submarines by virtue of her 31-knot top speed, and completed more than 600,000 miles in active service.

OCTOBER 12

'Naked Ape' Causes Furore

The British publishing world had a controversial new focal point today when *The Naked Ape* set tongues wagging at its launch. Written by Desmond Morris, who was until recently Curator of Mammals at London Zoo, it gave sociology a new slant by analyzing man's behaviour in terms of the animal kingdom in general and the ape family in particular.

As a trained zoologist, Morris had an extensive knowledge of animal behaviour which he believed could also be applied to his fellow humans who he described in the book as 'the sexiest primate alive'.

OCTOBER 9

Che Guevara Dies In Action

ERNESTO 'CHE' GUEVARA, the Argentine-born revolutionary who rejected both capitalist and mainstream communist systems to become the idol and poster pin-up of many a radical student during the 1960s, finally met his death today, at the hands of Bolivian Government forces.

Rumours of Che's death had been frequent since he 'disappeared' into South America two years earlier. But this time there was no doubt as Bolivian officials provided grisly evidence when they displayed his body at a news conference (pictured). He was 39 years old.

During those two 'missing' years, Guevara had been the champion of popular revolutionary movements throughout South America. A fervent supporter and trusted friend of Fidel Castro in his battle against Cuban dictator Batistá in the late 1950s, Guevara served under Castro as Deputy and as Minister of Industries before leaving to 'export' the Cuban revolution to other Latin American countries.

OCTOBER 18

Film Fun For Fab Four

The première of *How I Won The War,* which featured John Lennon's first serious film role, was held at London's Pavilion Theatre tonight. The Beatle had lost his locks to play the part of Private Gripweed in Richard Lester's anti-war comedy, which had been filmed in Germany and Spain in September last year.

The film, which also starred Michael Crawford and Roy Kinnear, was generally well received by the critics – a fate that would be denied *Magical Mystery Tour,* The Beatles' one-hour TV special, on its December TV screening.

Having postponed a planned visit to their guru, the Maharishi Mahesh Yogi, following the death of manager Brian Epstein, the group had spent a week in September cruising the highways and byways of England filming footage to create the surreal *Magical Mystery Tour,* songs from which would later be released on an album of the same name.

JUNE 10

SPENCER TRACY: THE FILM STARS' FILM STAR

More than any other actor, Spencer Tracy, who died today at his Hollywood home at the age of 67, was the epitome of the old-style US film star, bringing a luminosity and integrity to pretty well every role he tackled in his long, distinguished and award-strewn career.

That had begun on the New York stage in 1922, but from 1930 it was devoted entirely to the big screen. Originally cast either as a gangster or a tough, worldly priest by a studio system which recognized a great actor but figured someone with non-matinée looks had to be a bit of a 'heavy', he'd turned in two exceptional performances, in the 1932, film *One Thousand Years In Sing Sing* and *The Power And The Glory* a year later, before winning his first Best Actor Oscar in 1937 with the costume drama *Captains Courageous*.

At last realizing that Tracy could tackle just about any role with equal weight, conviction and ease, studio bosses allowed him to take on broader subjects, with the result that, in 1938, he won his second Academy Award for *Boys Town*.

A confirmed Roman Catholic, Tracy would never divorce his wife, although the undoubted love of his life - after they first met in the 1942 comedy *Woman Of The Year* - was Katharine Hepburn. It would be only the first of nine great films they would make together, their on-screen union culminating, just before Tracy died, with *Guess Who's Coming To Dinner*.

But it was the consummate skill which Tracy brought to the different challenges of vastly differing roles which made him extra special, and able to be included among the very few actors whose presence could make a good film great, and a great film a classic. Those classic appearances included *Northwest Passage* (1940), *State Of The Union* (1944), *Adam's Rib* (with Hepburn, in 1949), *Father Of The Bride* (1950), *Bad Day At Black Rock* (1955) and the 1960 production *Inherit The Wind*.

They just don't make 'em like Spencer Tracy any more.

JULY 21

ALBERT LUTHULI: CHAMPION OF FREEDOM

It was typical of the regime he fought with such dignity and courage for most of his life that the death today of Albert Luthuli, the 68-year-old Zulu chieftain who had led the African National Congress since 1952, was not officially confirmed by the South African Government until September this year. Even though they had confined Luthuli to a harsh exile in a remote part of the country in 1957 under rules which made it impossible to contact other ANC leaders legally, his death (reputedly under the wheels of a train) was still something the apartheid regime felt it had to keep secret for as long as it could.

A confirmed pacifist, despite the indignities heaped on him and his people, Luthuli was born in Bulawayo, was educated at a Methodist mission school and was a teacher for 15 years before becoming chief of the Abasemakholweni tribe in 1936 - a title the South African government stripped him of in 1956 when he was first charged with treason.

Although those charges were dropped, the authorities used the catch-all conditions of the Suppression of Communism Act to banish Luthuli, although he was never a member of the Communist Party!

A hero to many sympathetic bodies around the world, Luthuli was unable to travel to Scotland when students elected him Rector of Glasgow University, nor to Oslo in 1960 when he was awarded the Nobel Peace Prize - a fully deserved honour only confirmed by Luthuli's 1962 book *Let My People Go* which, while confirming his hostility to white repression, also stressed his continued rejection of black militancy.

JULY 17

JOHN COLTRANE: TAKING GIANT STEPS

Throughout a career marked by controversy, as contemporary music critics failed to keep up with his ability to make quantum leaps in what they perceived modern jazz to be, John Coltrane - who died today at the age of 41 - left a legacy of recordings which have not only withstood the passage of time, but still serve as a template for a generation of young sax players enthralled by his brilliance and inventiveness.

Born in North Carolina, Coltrane started his professional career in rhythm and blues groups, but by the early 1950s was working alongside trumpeter Dizzy Gillespie before becoming as important to the history-making mid-1950s Miles Davis Quintet as its trumpet-playing star.

After 18 months with Davis, Coltrane moved to a period with Thelonius Monk before moving out on his own to pursue of a style which consisted of 'sheets of sound' and reached a definitive stage with his two 1959 albums, *Giant Steps* and *Coltrane Jazz*.

A patron of free-form players like Archie Shepp, Pharoah Sanders and John Tchicai, Coltrane's own experiments with free-form jazz confused many, but in retrospect proved to be the definitive link between the Bebop era and the truly modern Modern Jazz still being explored by musicians who can only marvel at Coltrane's genius.

The Graduate Is Box-Office Sensation

SIMON AND GARFUNKEL'S hymn to *Mrs Robinson* celebrated the release of *The Graduate,* the comedy film of the year whose lightness of touch, courtesy of director Mike Nichols, turned it into an international box-office smash.

Anne Bancroft played the lady in question, a bored housewife who, after a few drinks, seduces a younger man who's not only her daughter's age but the son of two of her closest friends. But Benjamin Braddock, played by the unknown 30-year-old Dustin Hoffman, ran into bigger problems when his parents insisted he start dating Mrs Robinson's daughter Elaine (Katharine Ross).

While Bancroft – in reality not Mrs Robinson but Mrs Mel Brooks – didn't pick up an Oscar for her work, Mike Nichols did, while Simon and Garfunkel's soundtrack would go on to top the US chart for nine weeks, earning them a platinum record for more than a million sales.

NOVEMBER 7

Russians Show Full Force In Red Square

There was an unwanted reminder of the Cold War which still existed between East and West today in Moscow when Soviet armed forces mounted an unprecedented display of might to celebrate the 50th anniversary of the Russian Revolution.

The parade which passed through Red Square in front of the Kremlin, revealed five new types of missile. As Premier Brezhnev chillingly - and publicly - explained to visiting world communist leaders, the Soviet Union 'would not flinch' from employing them against any aggressors.

NOVEMBER 19

Prime Minister Wilson Devalues Pound

An attempt to halt the confusion which had reigned in the world's money markets for the last few days was made today in London when Prime Minister Harold Wilson announced that the pound would again be devalued against the dollar, dropping from $2.80 to $2.40.

The move meant that the PM had won his argument with Chancellor James Callaghan, who disagreed with the policy and had recently been quoted as saying that devaluation 'is a flight into escapism'. The value of the pound against its US counterpart now stood at its lowest since the beginning of the century.

Memorably, the Prime Minister attempted to soothe British alarm by saying, 'It does not mean, of course, that the pound here in Britain, in your pocket or purse, or in your bank, has been devalued.'

NOVEMBER 21

Foot And Mouth Devastates UK Farms

The greatest fear of every farmer must be the loss of all his livestock, and for many during the last few weeks their worst nightmares were confirmed as the dreaded foot and mouth disease ran rampant through the British countryside.

According to figures released in London today, 134,000 animals had already been slaughtered in the most devastating outbreak of the disease since 1923. And, despite the increasing numbers of herds being sacrificed, the disease showed no signs of abating.

A week later, the Jockey Club would be forced to suspend all horse-racing for the duration, and early in December the Government announced a ban on all meat from counties affected by the disease.

UK TOP 10 SINGLES

1: Baby, Now That I Found You
- The Foundations

2: Massachusetts
- The Bee Gees

3: Zabadak
- Dave Dee, Dozy, Beaky, Mick & Tich

4: Autumn Almanac
- The Kinks

5: The Last Waltz
- Engelbert Humperdinck

6: Love Is All Around
- The Troggs

7: From The Underworld
- The Herd

8: San Franciscan Nights
- Eric Burdon & The Animals

9: Homburg
- Procol Harum

10: There Is A Mountain
- Donovan

ARRIVALS

Born this month

4: Letitia Dean, UK television actress (*EastEnders*)

7: Sharleen Spiteri, UK pop singer (Texas)

17: Ronald DeVoe, US pop star (New Edition)

20: Stuart Ripley, UK football player

24: Gavin Maguire, UK football player

DEPARTURES

Died this month:

9: Charles Bickford, US film actor (*The Big Country, Johnny Belinda, A Star Is Born,* etc), TV star (*The Virginian* series), aged 78

12: Dorothy Laverne Good, US country singer (*Girls Of The Golden West*)

20: Casimir Funk, Polish-born US biochemist (inventor of the word 'vitamin'), aged 83

NOVEMBER 14

Philby Comes In From the Cold

Kim Philby (pictured), the British spy who defected to Russia four years ago, finally ended the silence which had surrounded him since, and gave his first interview to Western journalists in Moscow today.

Philby, like Anthony Blunt, Guy Burgess and Donald Maclean, was converted to communism during his time at Trinity College Cambridge in the 1930s and recruited there by the KGB in 1933. Six years later, upon the outbreak of war, he joined MI6 and for a large part of the next 24 years held key posts which allowed him access to top secret information.

Although Burgess and Maclean were rumbled in the early 1950s, Philby managed to stay one step ahead of his masters and the CIA, defecting just before he was about to be arrested. Breaking his silence now paved the way for publication of his revealing book, *My Silent War,* in 1968.

NOVEMBER 9

Rock Journalism Comes Of Age

THE FIRST ISSUE OF US rock magazine *Rolling Stone* was published today in San Francisco. Founded by Jann Wenner, a former student of the University of California, with encouragement from veteran jazz critic Ralph J Gleason, its aim was to report on rock as an enduring art form rather than ephemeral entertainment, and also to report on the culture that created it.

Unlike Britain, there had previously been no nationally-distributed US music magazine that addressed the rock audience rather than the music industry, and with musical creativity at an all-time high the publication found a ready readership.

By the 1980s, *Rolling Stone* would have worldwide sales of over 800,000, had left its San Francisco home for New York and would no longer be an 'alternative' newspaper. Even so, some of rock's most enduring images - the naked John Lennon with Yoko Ono in foetal crouch, for instance - would reach the world via its pages.

NOVEMBER 9

Haitink Joins London Philharmonic

The London Philharmonic Orchestra, founded in 1932 by the great Sir Thomas Beecham, gave its first concert with its new principal conductor, Bernard Haitink, this evening. Haitink took the place on the podium of John Pritchard, who had held the post for the past five years.

The LPO's new maestro came with excellent credentials, having spent more than 10 years with the renowned Concertgebouw Orchestra in his home city, Amsterdam. He specialized in the symphonic works of Bruckner and Mahler. He had made his US concert début in 1958, and his first British appearance a year later.

NOVEMBER 30

Aid Row As Britain Quits Aden

Since before the birth of Christ, the port of Aden on the tip of the Arabian Peninsula had been a crucial link for trade between the Indian Ocean and the Mediterranean - and it had formed part of the British Empire for the past 128 years.

All that changed today when British troops were hastily evacuated from South Yemen, under fire from the country's new leader, Qantan al-Shaabi, who accused Britain of reneging on a deal to provide his regime with £58 million-worth of aid.

In the end, the rebels - who had been waging a liberation campaign in the colony for the past four years - settled for £10 million, together with the preservation of diplomatic ties with their former rulers.

DECEMBER 3

Triumph For Barnard, Human Heart-Swap Pioneer

THE FIRST PATIENT to receive another human heart grinned triumphantly and posed with nurses at Groote Shuur Hospital in Cape Town, South Africa, today - the benificiary of pioneering surgery carried out by a team of 30 headed by surgeon Dr Christiaan Barnard (pictured).

Louis Washkansky was a 53-year-old dying of heart disease when Denise Darvall, a 25-year-old road crash victim, agreed to her heart being used by Dr Barnard. She also donated her kidneys to a black boy in another hospital.

Behind the smiles for photographers, Mr Washkansky knew that the otherwise successful operation would not save his life, and he died of lung problems related to tissue rejection on December 21.

The ground-breaking pioneer, Dr Barnard, had trained in the United States. Until today, the only heart transplants had been carried out on animals. His achievement led the way for a revolution in transplant surgery.

DECEMBER 10

Soul Star Otis Redding Killed

Otis Redding, the legendary US soul singer and songwriter, died today when the plane in which he was travelling between concert engagements crashed into the waters of Lake Monoma, Wisconsin. He was aged 26 and had just begun to establish himself with a large white US rock audience after his triumph at the Monterey Pop festival in the summer.

Four members of his touring band, The Bar Kays – James King, Ronald Caldwell, Phalon Jones and Carl Cunningham – died along with him. Rush-released only days after the crash, his *(Sittin' On) The Dock Of The Bay* would become his only single to top the US pop chart, although he had enjoyed numerous hits and widespread popularity in Britain and Europe before his death.

Fellow soul singers Joe Tex, Joe Simon, Johnnie Taylor, Solomon Burke, Percy Sledge, Don Covay and Sam Moore were pall bearers at his funeral at the City Auditorium in his home-town of Macon, Georgia, indicating the regard in which Redding was held.

DECEMBER 9

Doors Singer Arrested On Stage

Police arrested controversial rock shaman Jim Morrison today as his group, The Doors, played a New Haven, Connecticut, concert. He had earlier been involved in an altercation with a policeman, who responded by spraying him with Mace, a type of tear gas. On stage, in the middle of *Back Door Man,* Morrison delivered his impression of the incident, at which point the police turned on the house lights, stopped the performance and arrested the singer on the double charge of a breach of the peace and resisting arrest.

DECEMBER 17

Australian Prime Minister Lost At Sea

All hope of finding the Prime Minister of Australia, Harold Holt, alive faded today. He was believed to have drowned while swimming in the ocean near his home in Victoria. Rescue services mounted a huge search operation along thirty miles of coastline but found no trace of Mr Holt, who was a keen diver. His deputy, John McEwen, was appointed to replace him.

Harold Holt had been Prime Minister since 1966, when he took over from Robert Menzies, and would probably be remembered most for his slogan in support of the US President's stance on Vietnam, 'All the way with LBJ'.

UK TOP 10 SINGLES

1: Hello Goodbye
- The Beatles

2: If The Whole World Stopped Loving
- Val Doonican

3: Let The Heartaches Begin
- Long John Baldry

4: Something's Gotten Hold Of My Heart
- Gene Pitney

5: I'm Comin' Home
- Tom Jones

6: Everybody Knows
- The Dave Clark Five

7: All My Love
- Cliff Richard

8: Careless Hands
- Des O'Connor

9: Daydream Believer
- The Monkees

10: World
- The Bee Gees

ARRIVALS

Born this month:

7: David Hirst, UK football player.

DEPARTURES

Died this month:

10: Otis Redding, US Soul singer and songwriter *(see main story)*, aged 26

29: Paul Whiteman, US orchestra leader, aged 77

31: Bert Berns, US pop songwriter, producer and talent spotter, aged 38

DECEMBER 11

Concorde Unveiled With Show Of Accord

THE WORLD HAD ITS first glimpse of *Concorde* (pictured with chief test pilot Brian Trubshaw), the Anglo-French supersonic airliner, today when it rolled majestically out of its hangar at Toulouse. The successful completion of this joint project was all the more amazing in view of the continued climate of disagreement between the two nations, although there had been an unseemly row over whether the aircraft's name should be spelt with a final 'e'.

Sixteen of the world's airlines had taken options to buy the airliner, but only Air France and British Airways, the national carriers of the two countries concerned, actually went on to buy and operate the type, which remained the world's only supersonic passenger transport in the 1990s.

DECEMBER 21

'Half A Sixpence' Opens In London

The film of the hit stage musical *Half A Sixpence* opened tonight in London with its original star – Tommy Steele – in the lead role. Launched with the slogan, 'It's everything a motion picture can be', Paramount were hoping that Steele, who played the cockney draper's assistant on stage between 1963 and 1964, would also wow the world's cinema audiences.

The pop bandwagon had rolled on as Steele, one of Britain's first home-produced rock'n'rollers in the late 1950s, diversified to become an all-round entertainer. He would, however, endure as a modern-day song and dance man, playing the lead at the London Palladium in the 1980s in *Singing In The Rain* and touring with his own show, featuring hits from other stage successes, in the 1990s.

DECEMBER 31

King Constantine Flees To Italy

An ill-advised counter coup by King Constantine of Greece ended before it had begun today when expected support within the Greek armed forces failed to materialize. Colonel Papadopoulos, leader of the junta which itself seized power just eight months ago, said he believed the King must have been misled by what he called 'power seekers' within the armed forces, labelling the failed coup as a 'criminal conspiracy'.

The King fled with his family to Italy, aware that, back home in Greece, neither right nor left of the political divide seemed to have a good word to say about him.

DECEMBER 14

Wimbledon Defies World To Admit Professionals

Britain's Lawn Tennis Association defied threats of suspension from the international game in London today when an overwhelming majority of its members voted to end the distinction between amateurs and professionals in lawn tennis from the start of the 1968 season.

Only five members voted against ratifying the Association's management committee's decision of last month, which meant that from April 22 - when the Bournemouth hard-court championships were scheduled to start - players would be called just that, regardless of whether they usually played for money or not.

YOUR 1967 HOROSCOPE

Unlike most Western horoscope systems which group astrological signs into month-long periods based on the influence of 12 constellations, the Chinese believe that those born in the same year of their calendar share common qualities, traits and weaknesses with one of 12 animals - Rat, Ox, Tiger, Rabbit, Dragon, Snake, Horse, Sheep, Monkey, Rooster, Dog or Pig.

They also allocate the general attributes of five natural elements - Earth, Fire, Metal, Water, Wood - and an overall positive or negative aspect to each sign to summarize its qualities.

If you were born between January 21, 1966 and February 8, 1967, you are a Horse. As this book is devoted to the events of 1967, let's take a look at the sign which governs those born between February that year and January 29, 1968 - The Year of The Sheep:

THE SHEEP

FEBRUARY 9, 1967 - JANUARY 29, 1968

ELEMENT: WOOD ASPECT: (-)

Sheep are socially, domestically and politically correct people, happy with the status quo, respect order and generally obey the rules and regulations society lays down.

The Year of the Sheep is characterized as a time of relative peace and tranquility because Sheep need harmony and usually go with the flow to maintain that harmony, contenting themselves with the concensus and playing the game.

Sheep have strong inherent herding instincts and function best as a part of a team, and members of that group lack individuality. Politically speaking, the Sheep is the sign of the moderate and the democrat, and it's precisely by keeping their heads and opinions down that Sheep manage to withstand and survive the many ups and downs of life.

Fortune favours the Sheep, possibly because they are so mild and unassuming they wouldn't be capable of using their own efforts and endeavours to make their own fortune. Consequently, luck helps make for an easy life where Sheep are concerned. If they are in public life, Sheep would be wise to have a reliable agent or manager to protect and promote them.

Sheep are tidy and appreciate ordered life and work environments. Males are particularly courteous and chivalrous, adhering to old-fashioned gentlemanly codes. However, while being passive and unoriginal creatures, they do like to show off - under a spotlight they can't resist turning into performers and showmen.

The sign of the Sheep is the most feminine and passive of all, and many female Sheep master and shine in arts and crafts. They have a keen eye for beauty and simply adore exquisite things. Psychologically, they need to be surrounded by beauty, for without pleasant and conducive surroundings they easily become depressed and dispirited.

It is essential for a Sheep - male and female - that they create a warm, harmonious and united domestic environment for themselves.

FAMOUS SHEEP

Muhammad Ali
former world heavyweight boxing champion

Boris Becker
German tennis player

Ian Botham
English cricket player

Terence Conran
British design guru, restaurateur

Catherine Deneuve
French film actress

John Denver
US singer, actor

Mikhail Gorbachev
former Russian leader

Mick Jagger
singer, songwriter, actor

Billie-Jean King
US tennis player, coach

James Michener
novelist